Indigenous Sa~~~
and Spiritual (

M000296930

Since time immemorial, indigenous people have engaged in legal relationships with other-than-human persons. These relationships are exemplified in enspirited sacred natural sites, which are owned and governed by numina spirits that can potentially place legal demands on humankind in return for protection and blessing. Although conservationists recognise the biodiverse significance of most sacred natural sites, the role of spiritual agency by other-than-human persons is not well understood. Consequently, sacred natural sites typically lack legal status and IUCN-designated protection. More recent ecocentric and posthuman worldviews and polycentric legal frameworks have allowed courts and legislatures to grant 'rights' to nature and 'juristic personhood' and standing to biophysical entities. This book examines the indigenous literature and recent legal cases as a pretext for granting juristic personhood to enspirited sacred natural sites.

The author draws on two decades of his research among Tibetans in Kham (southwest China), to provide a detailed case study. It is argued that juristic personhood is contingent upon the presence and agency of a resident numina and that recognition should be given to their role in spiritual governance over their jurisdiction. The book concludes by recommending that advocacy organisations help indigenous people with test cases to secure standing for threatened sacred natural sites (SNS) and calls upon IUCN, UNESCO (MAB and WHS), ASEAN Heritage and EuroNatura to retrospectively re-designate their properties, reserves, parks and initiatives so that SNS and spiritual governance are fully recognised and embraced.

It will be of great interest to advanced students and researchers in environmental law, nature conservation, religion and anthropology.

John Studley is an Independent Ethno-forestry Researcher and consultant, with many years of experience in the UK, China and Nepal.

Routledge Focus on Environment and Sustainability

Jainism and Environmental Philosophy
Karma and the Web of Life
Aidan Rankin

Social Sustainability, Climate Resilience and Community-Based Urban Development
What About the People?
Cathy Baldwin and Robin King

South Africa's Energy Transition
A Roadmap to a Decarbonised, Low-cost and Job-rich Future
Tobias Bischof-Niemz and Terence Creamer

The Environmental Sustainable Development Goals in Bangladesh
Edited by Samiya A. Selim, Shantanu Kumar Saha, Rumana Sultana and Carolyn Roberts

Climate Change Discourse in Russia
Past and Present
Edited by Marianna Poberezhskaya and Teresa Ashe

The Greening of US Free Trade Agreements
From NAFTA to the Present Day
Linda J. Allen

Indigenous Sacred Natural Sites and Spiritual Governance
The Legal Case for Juristic Personhood
John Studley

For more information about this series, please visit: www.routledge.com/ Routledge-Focus-on-Environment-and-Sustainability/book-series/RFES

Indigenous Sacred Natural Sites and Spiritual Governance

The Legal Case for Juristic Personhood

John Studley

Routledge
Taylor & Francis Group
LONDON AND NEW YORK

from Routledge

First published 2019 by Routledge

2 Park Square, Milton Park, Abingdon, Oxfordshire OX14 4RN

52 Vanderbilt Avenue, New York, NY 10017

Routledge is an imprint of the Taylor & Francis Group, an informa business

First issued in paperback 2020

British Library Cataloguing-in-Publication Data
A catalogue record for this book is available from the British Library

Library of Congress Cataloging-in-Publication Data
Names: Studley, John.
Title: Indigenous sacred natural sites and spiritual governance :
    the legal case of juristic personhood/John Studley.
Description: Abingdon, Oxon; New York, NY : Routledge, 2019. |
    Includes bibliographical references and index.
Identifiers: LCCN 2018033494 (print) | LCCN 2018038099 (ebook) |
    ISBN 9780429455797 (eBook) | ISBN 9781138316232 (hb)
Subjects: LCSH: Sacred space – Law and legislation. | Protected areas –
    Law and legislation. | Juristic persons. | Locus standi. | Nature –
    Religious aspects. | Indigenous peoples (International law)
Classification: LCC K3791 (ebook) | LCC K3791 .S78 2019 (print) |
    DDC 344/.094 – dc23
LC record available at https://lccn.loc.gov/2018033494

ISBN: 978-1-138-31623-2 (hbk)
ISBN: 978-0-367-60666-4 (pbk)

Typeset in Times New Roman
by Apex CoVantage, LLC

To עליון and the mountain peoples of northwest Nepal and southwest China who taught me new ways of knowing and new ways of being

Contents

Figures and tables

Figures

Tables

Preface

This book was triggered by three events in my life: a serendipitous epiphany on the Tibetan Plateau in 1999, an incredulous reaction to 'spiritless' assumptions made about the 'governance' of sacred natural sites (SNS) in the Kawakarpo Mountain Range (northwest Yunnan) in 2013, and fortuitous legislation in 2017.

The epiphany occurred while I was conducting research in the Upper Yangtze in 1999. I asked a Tibetan farmer if there was a connection between environmental care and his spiritual beliefs, and he responded in the following way:

> If we protect (and nurture) the abode (the middle slopes of a local mountain) and property (bio-physical resources) of 'Jo Bo' (meaning Lord, ruler and elder brother in Tibetan), he will be happy and bless us with good health, good crop yields, and wise leadership. If not he will be angry and cause sickness, calamity, crop failure and disaster upon us and our community.

The farmer went on to describe the role of *Jo Bo*, the resources and villages he had jurisdiction over and the geospatial extents of his mountain fastness, which corresponds to a sacred natural site.

It took time to identify that *Jo Bo* was a *numen* (*gzhi bdag* in Tibetan) and is classified on the basis of Tibetan scholarship under the aegis of *mi-chos* or the "religion of men" (Stein, 1972: 192). It was, however, possible to draw some tentative observations from the discussion with the farmer. The 'cult of *Jo Bo*' is a distinctive expression of the Animistic cultural pole of Tibetan lay society, which is differentiated from the Tibetan Buddhist pole (Karmay, 1998) and is predicated on contractual reciprocity (between villagers and *Jo Bo*).

Jo Bo appears to be both owner and custodian of his mountain domain and its biophysical resources and is seemingly solely responsible for its care. *Jo Bo*'s jurisdiction is normative, administrative and territorial, and the associated *sui generis* norms are recognised by local people and his personhood is made manifest to them through anthropomorphic characteristics and kinship title. The protection and nurturance of *Jo Bo*'s domain appear to result in biodiverse habitats and the act of ritual protection to be an exemplar of behaviour that mimics explicit environmental protection.

It took further research (1999–2005 and 2013) to establish that the comments made by the farmer in 1999 were not a 'one-off'. In reality, enspirited SNS and the *gzhi bdag* cult appears to be part of a pattern of behaviour that is common across the lay Tibetan world and among Indigenous people (Studley, 2005, 2014).

After conducting a biocultural audit of enspirited SNS in the Kawakarpo Mountains in 2013, I participated in an online discussion group on a conservation forum. The discussants were all very keen to hear about my findings, but I was perplexed when they asked me to describe the 'governance' of the SNS (inhabited and owned by *numina*). I did not know how to respond given that IUCN governance categories are solely predicated on human agency. As a result, I told them about the land immediately adjacent to the SNS where governance is under the aegis of the village headmen and predicated on locally agreed rules.

The discussion raised important questions in my mind about the anthropocentric and 'godless' nature of the governance typology used by some conservation organisations and their exogenous *modus operandi*. I began to explore alternative forms of governance by other-than-human persons (Hallowell, 1960: 22), and I encountered the term "spiritual governance" (Bellezza, 1997: 41), which I co-opted because it was evident as a behavioural interactive practice between humans and their *numina* (Studley, 2005).

Furthermore, I explored the legal status of spirits and *numina* and discovered that juristic personhood and standing was granted to enspirited idols by colonial judges in India in the early 1900s (*Mullick v. Mullick*, 1925), UK judges in 1991 (*Bumper v. Met. Police*, 1991), and Indian Judges as recently as 2010 (*Akhara v. Lord Ram*, 2010) – where Lord Ram was the plaintiff.

I did not have to argue for juristic personhood for enspirited landscapes, as fortuitously others did it for me. The new legislation, mostly in 2017, granted juristic personhood and standing to Indigenous homelands, rivers and their catchments in New Zealand, India and Colombia.

The legislation, which resonated with the "posthuman turn" (Clarke and Rossini, 2016: 143), developments in "pluriversality" (James, 1977) and "late modern law" (Modéer, 2016: 62), provided me with an apposite conceptual and legal framework to defend sacred natural sites *in toto*. It enabled me to argue that sacred natural sites and their resident 'spirits of place' should also be granted juristic personhood and standing and that the role of spirits in spiritual governance should be recognised in law.

I have written on the subject of the juristic personhood of enspirited SNS and the spiritual governance of SNS but was not able to fully explore the topic in a journal format. I was encouraged to write this book by Bas Verschuuren in order to do justice to the subject. I begin with the rationale for protecting SNS emanating from research in Tibet (Chapter 1). I subsequently go on to explain the conceptual basis for non-anthropocentric approaches to nature (Chapter 2) before exploring the spiritual ecology of the Indigenous people who typically protect most enspirited landscapes (Chapter 3) as a platform to explain the importance and legal basis of Juristic Personhood (Chapter 4), illustrated with pertinent legislation (Chapter 5), examples of litigation (Chapter 6), and a case study from Tibet, which provides the behavioural context for the ritual protection of SNS (Chapter 7). The book concludes with the challenges of perpetuating SNS (Chapter 8) and of prosecuting them (Chapter 9).

Acknowledgements

The author would like to thank the following for their comments and contributions: William (Bill) Bleisch, Sabine Brels, Robyn Duncan, Shibani Ghosh, Liza Higgins-Zogib, Peter Horsley, Harry Jonas, Joseph Lambert, Philip Lyver, Paul Sochaczewski, Bas Verschuuren, three anonymous reviewers, one commissioning editor and the copy editor.

Abbreviations

ABN	African Biodiversity Network
ACHPR	African Commission on Human and Peoples' Rights
BLNR	Board of Land and Natural Resources (Hawaii)
CELDF	Community Environmental Legal Defence Fund
CRIC	Consejo Regional Indígena del Cauca (Colombia)
DBH	Diameter at breast height (1.3 m for trees)
DNA	Deoxyribonucleic acid
DPGEL	Director de la Procuraduria General Del Estadode Loja (Ecuador)
GF	Gaia Foundation
GT	Grant township
KAHEA	Ka (the) Hawaiian-Environmental Alliance
ICCA	Indigenous Community Conserved Areas
ICJ	International Commission of Jurists
ISNS	Indigenous sacred natural site
IUCN	International Union for the Conservation of Nature
MKAH	Mauna Kea Anaina Hou (Hawaii)
NGO	Non-government organization
NIT	Ngā Iwi o Taranaki (New Zealand)
OECM	Other effective area-based conservation measures
OIA	Organización Indígena de Antioquia (Colombia)
PAs	Protected areas (IUCN recognised)
PGE	Pennsylvania General Energy Company
PNG	Papua New Guinea
REANCBRN	Republica del Ecuador Asamblea Nacional Comision de la Biodiversidad y Recursos Naturales (Ecuador)
ROU	Record of understanding
SNS	Sacred natural site
TAP	Tibetan Autonomous Prefecture
TB	Tibetan Buddhism

UHH	University of Hawaii Hilo
UNDRIP	United Nations Declaration on the Rights of Indigenous Peoples
UNESCAP	United Nations Economic and Social Commission for Asia and the Pacific
USA	United States of America
WCC	World Council of Churches
WHS	World Heritage Status

Biodata

Dr John Studley is an independent ethno-forestry researcher, a Chartered Geographer, a fellow of the Royal Geographic Society and an international fellow of the Explorers Club. He has a PhD in ethno-forestry, an MA in Rural Social Development and diplomas in forestry, cross-cultural studies and theology. He has spent most of his working life among and learning from the mountain peoples of High Asia, and has spent the last five years researching Indigenous sacred natural sites among the Tibetan people of southwest China. In recognition of his research, he has recently become an honorary member of the Indigenous Community Conserved Area consortium and a member of Spiritual and Cultural Values of Protected Areas working group of IUCN.

Key Terms

agency		Agency is the capacity of an 'actor' (human or non-human) to act in any given environment or social structure
bdag po	བདག་པོ།	Literally meaning the 'master of all the different beings' – lord, master, owner, proprietor, spouse, husband, a companion for life, dominance, environment, boss, proprietor, owner, guardian
bon or *bon chos*	བོན་ཆོས།	The 'bon religion' is a Tibetan religion, which self-identifies as distinct from Tibetan Buddhism, although it shares the same overall teachings and terminology.
bsang yig	བསང་ཡི།	'sang yig' is a ritual written liturgy – 'Sang' is the name of a ritual in which smoke is made in a ritual fire and offered up. Doing this cleanses, sanctifies and brings blessing to the people and places involved. 'Yig' means letter, writing[s]. {yi ge}, manual, syllable, letter
bskog zhag	བསྐོད་ཞག།	To designate
byin brlabs	བྱིན་བརླབས།	Blessing or consecration of trees or plants
comity of nations		The informal and voluntary recognition by courts of one jurisdiction of the laws and judicial decisions of another

cosmoscape		"A culture's overarching model and template of the shape and scope of the cosmos is a representation and a shared imagery of the visual form of the universe and of the structure and function of the whole universe or cosmos" (Reichel, 2012: 136–137)
de facto		In law and government, *de facto* describes practices that exist in reality, even if not legally recognised by official laws.
de jure		By right or according to the law (distinguished from de facto)
'dul ba	འདུལ་བ།	The basic meaning is to take something which has a behaviour that is coarse or undesirable or not in accord with reality or not in accord with some desired mode and to modify it, adjust it, train it, break it in, so that it now behaves in a way that is desired, needed, in accord with reality, or in accord with some desired mode.
enspirited or enspiriting		Enspiriting is a ritual (and sometimes liturgical) process whereby a spirit or *numina* is 'called down' by Animistic humankind and invited to inhabit a biophysical entity (mountain, forest, rock, idol), which becomes enspirited permanently providing the spirit is honoured and appeased on a regular basis.
epistemic (landscapes)	from Greek *epistēmē* 'knowledge'	Epistemic landscapes (in this context) are visionary, virtual, imagined or contrived by Tibetan Buddhism/Bonpo (Huber, 1999) and are characterised by the de-wilding, de-souling, subjugation and re-mapping of nature (McKay, 2013) and are "devoid of ontic substance" (Tacey, 2013: 139).

ethnojurisprudence		Is predicated on the study of the law, anthropology, ethnology, political science, sociology and human relations (Zion, 1988)
ethnojurists		Intercultural communicator, a reconciler of values, a fixer, an arranger, an author, a factotum and many other things (Zion, 1988)
FIR		First Information Report (FIR) is a written document prepared by the police when they receive information about the commission of a cognisable offence.
genius loci		In classical Roman religion, a *genius loci* (plural *genii loci*) was the protective spirit of a place.
gnas	གནས།	'ne' – to abide; dwell; source; state; situation; remain; last; stay; place; abode; topic; object; retention
guardian *ad litum*		(Guardian appointed by a court) is someone appointed by the court to represent a client for the duration of a particular legal action
gzhi bdag	གཞི་བདག	'shi da' – local deity, local guardians. local spirits; master of the locality; local protective deities; genius loci.
in loco parentis	From the Latin 'in place of a parent'	Refers to the legal requirement of a person (or persons) to take on the responsibilities of a parent for another entity
intervenor		In law, intervention is a procedure to allow a nonparty, called intervenor (also spelt intervener), to join ongoing litigation, either as a matter of right or at the discretion of the court, without the permission of the original litigants.
'jig rten pa'i srung ma	འཇིག་རྟེན་པའི་སྲུང་མ།	A class of mundane deities and protectors who belong to the phenomenal world

jus gentium	From the Latin 'law of nations'	A concept of international law within the ancient Roman legal system and Western law traditions based on or influenced by it. The *jus gentium* is not a body of statute law or a legal code, but rather customary law thought to be held in common by all *gentes* ('peoples' or 'nations') in reasoned compliance with standards of international conduct.
kora	སྐོར་ར།	'Kora' is a transliteration of a Tibetan word that means 'circumambulation' or 'revolution'.
la btsas	ལ་བཙས།	A 'latse' is a cairn formed by heaps of stones in which poles bearing wind horse flags are put up in honour of the local deities.
legal positivism		Legal positivism is a philosophy of law that emphasises the conventional nature of law – that it is socially constructed.
lha pa	ལྷ་པ།	A trance medium with an indwelling spirit
limen (liminal)	Transliterated from the Greek Λιμήν for refuge	A threshold
ma chags pa	མ་ཆགས་པ།	Non-attachment is one of the eleven virtuous mental states – desirelessness, not being attached, without attachment.
mandalized (mountains)	From the Sanskrit मण्डल	A mountain that has been re-mapped in order to transform it into a symbol of the realm of the Buddha and that is entirely sacralised by TB exercises.
matrilineal		Matrilineality is the tracing of descent through the female line.

mchod rten	མཆོད་རྟེན།	A 'chorten' is a stupa, pagoda, funeral monument, receptacle of offerings, masonry monuments, holder or depository for oblations.
mgon mam	མགོན་མམ།	'Mgon mam' is the abbreviation for *nyag rong mgon po mam rgyal*, a warlord who tried to unify Kham in the 19th century.
mi chos	མི་ཆོས།	Tradition, customs ways of men, customs and usages of common men or householders, householder, the religion of man
Mithraism		Mithraism, the worship of Mithra, the Iranian god of the sun, justice, contract and war in pre-Zoroastrian Iran.
modus operandi		*Modus operandi* is a Latin phrase, approximately translated as method or mode of operating.
monism	from Greek *monos* 'single'	Monism is defined as the view that reality is a unified whole and that all existing things can be ascribed to, or described by, a single concept or system.
monophasic		'monophasic' cultures regard the five physical senses and beta consciousness as the only valid ways of knowing and being
natural law		An observable law relating to natural phenomena
numina	From the Latin *Nūmen*	A *numen* is a 'spirit of place' or *genius loci* that is present within an object or place (mountain, forest, spring, idol).
ontic (landscapes)	From Ancient Greek ὄv (ón, 'being, existing, essence')	Ontic landscapes are real and experienced by laypeople on the basis of cult participation, autochthony and belonging (Lightfoot, 1986; Eliade, 1959).

pantheistic monism		Pantheistic monism identifies God with the universe and all that is in it.
parens patriae	From the Latin 'parents of the nation'	A public policy power of the state to intervene as legal guardian of an entity in need of protection
pho brang	ཕོ་བྲང་།	A castle, mansion, court, house, dwelling, or hall
phyi rgyal srung skyob	ཕྱི་རྒྱལ་སྲུང་སྐྱོབ།	Foreign defence (conservation)
polyphasic		Polyphasic cultures regard multiple senses (typically eight) and multiple states of consciousness (such as dreams, trance, visions, yogic, shamanic, psychoactive, entheogenic, non-egoic, contemplative and meditative states) as valid ways of knowing and being.
Ram	In Sanskrit or Devanagari राम	Rama or Ram is also known as Ramachandra, and is a major deity of Hinduism.
ri bsher	རི་བཤེར།	Mountain or hill inspectors
ri rgya	རི་རྒྱ།	A demarcation line on a mountain/hill denoting a prohibition on killing wild animals
ris med (movement)	རིས་མེད།	The movement's name is derived from two Tibetan words: *Ris* (bias, side) and *Med* (lack), which combined expresses the idea of openness to other Tibetan Buddhist traditions, as opposed to sectarianism. Rimé is intended to recognise the differences between traditions and appreciate them, while also establishing a dialogue which would create common ground.
rtsi shing tshe thar	རྩི་ཤིང་ཚེ་ཐར།	The custom of freeing or saving the lives of animals or in this case trees

sauvistika	卍	The *sauvistika* is a counter-clockwise cursive swastika and is synonymous with *yungdrung bon*,
sbas yul	སྦས་ཡུལ།	A 'beyul' is hidden country or land (a kind of earthly paradise with peaceful and blessed landscapes), which Padmasambhava blessed as refuges.
skyong	སྐྱོང།	To guard, keep, maintain, protect, nurture
snod bcud do mnyam	སྣོད་བཅུད་དོ་མཉམ	Keeping the container world and its contents in balance (or in topocosmic equilibrium)
srung skyob	སྲུང་སྐྱོབ།	Guard and protect, safeguard, defend
standing	From the Latin *locus standi*	In law, standing is the term for the ability of a party to demonstrate to the court sufficient connection to and harm from the law or action challenged to support that party's participation in the case.
statist		A political system in which the state has substantial centralised control over social and economic affairs.
stay		A stay of proceedings is a ruling by the court in civil and criminal procedure, halting further legal process in a trial or other legal proceeding. The court can subsequently lift the stay and resume proceedings based on events taking place after the stay is ordered.
subtractability		Economists recognise toll goods and common pool resources, which can be catalogued by two attributes: excludability and subtractability. They refer to subtractability as 'rivalness'. Essentially, the concept refers to how much of the good is left after consumption.

sui generis	Pronounced soo-ee jen-ris	Latin for 'of its own kind' and used to describe a form of legal protection that exists outside typical legal protections – that is, something that is unique or different.
sunyata	སྟོང་པ་ཉིད།	A key Buddhist concept used to express that everything one encounters in life is empty of absolute identity, permanence or an indwelling 'self'
taboos	In Polynesian *tabu* In Māori *tapu*	*Tapu* expresses the "process of setting a location aside to serve as a ritually protected space" (Issitt and Main, 2014: 454) and are invisible examples of informal institutions and norms.
tumuli	From the Latin *tumulus*	"Hillock, a heap of earth, mound"
Xia		The Xia dynasty (c. 2070–c. 1600 BC) is the first dynasty in traditional Chinese history. It is described in the Bamboo Annals and was established by the legendary Yu the Great.
yul lha	ཡུལ་ལྷ།	Regional deity
yungdrung bon	གཡུང་དྲུང་བོན།	Yungdrung Bon has a celestial and mystical orientation predicated on the *sauvastika*, the moon, the feminine, Mithraism and gnostic advancement or *sgo-phug-pa*.

1 Indigenous sacred natural sites with reference to Tibet

Sacred natural sites are found on six continents and in most countries. Some of them are seemingly among the oldest and most revered places on Earth, and concurrently new sacred natural sites are still being established, in some cases by migrants to new countries. Paleo-anthropological evidence indicates that early humans respected and honoured their ancestors at burial sites over 60,000 years ago. The honouring of ancestors and veneration of burial grounds seem to be a common trait of every culture of modern humans, as well as the reverence of natural features of great significance such as high mountains or large rivers.

Some Australian sacred sites appear to be at least 50,000 years old (Olsen, 2000); sacred rock art found in caves at Lascaux, France (Johanson and Edgar, 1996) date from 20,000 years ago; and some sacred *tumuli*, such as Glastonbury Tor[1] (Figure 1.1), date from 5,000 years ago.

At a landscape level, anthropologists have long recognised the unique status that cultures have given to nature not only in specific sacred sites (e.g., Frazer, 1890) but also in larger areas of cultural significance extending to entire landscapes. There has been an increasing recognition of the importance of sacred sites within the last twenty years, which has contributed to the exploration of new paradigms which have informed our understanding and the conservation of sacred natural sites (Posey, 1999).

1.1 Sacred natural site: an overview

Sacred natural sites are natural features or areas of land or water having special spiritual significance to peoples and communities (Wild and McLeod, 2008). This working definition is broad and can be used as a basis for more specific articulations, including sacred site, sacred place and sacred area.

The interest in sacred natural sites from the perspective of nature conservation lies in the components of biological diversity that they harbour, such as the species of animals and plants, the habitats and ecosystems,

Figure 1.1 Glastonbury Tor, England – a modified sacred natural site dating from Neolithic times

(By Laika ac from UK – CC-BY-SA 2.0)[2]

as well as the ecological dynamics and functions that support life within and outside the places. Linked to such biological diversity is the array of distinct human cultures that care for them and hold them sacred (Verschuuren et al., 2010).

Sacred natural sites consist of all types of natural features including mountains, hills, forests, groves, rivers, lakes, lagoons, caves, islands and springs. They can vary in size from the very small – an individual tree, small spring or a single rock formation – to whole landscapes and mountain ranges. They consist of geological formations, distinct landforms, specific ecosystems and natural habitats. They are predominantly terrestrial but are also found in inshore marine areas, islands and archipelagos.

Many sacred natural sites have been well protected over long time periods and have seen low levels of human utilisation. Many are demonstrably high in biodiversity and represent a strong biodiversity conservation opportunity (Dudley et al., 2009). Sacred natural sites are also predicated on ancient and profound cultural values. The behaviour of those who ritually protect ISNS from harm are expressions of the dedicated efforts by Indigenous or local people who have specifically, if not always consciously, cared for nature because of its inherent spiritual qualities in various ways.

Given that this book is juxtaposed between academic and popular discourse and ethnography, predicated on the author's research on the Tibetan plateau, it is important to provide the reader with some understanding of ISNS in the context of Animistic Tibetan culture.

1.2 The sacred natural sites of Tibet

Since time immemorial, much of Tibet's mountain landscapes have been inhabited and "enspirited" (Yü, 2015: 26) by deities known as *gzhi bdag* in Tibetan. The term 'en-spirited' is used deliberately to describe biophysical entities that are inhabited by a *numina* spirit or *genius loci*. It is used in preference to inspirited, animated or vivified because it describes a process that is contingent on human agency. Furthermore, the prefix 'en-' denotes conversion from one state to another, in this case from natural to enspirited.

These spirits (or *numina*) have been a defining cultural feature of Tibetan lay society. Their terrestrial abodes demarcated by a *la btsas* (Figure 1.2) are Indigenous sacred natural sites (ISNS) that are exemplars of human behaviour that mimics explicit nature conservation and protection norms. The Animistic beliefs that support the ritual protection of ISNS are typically referred to in the literature as "mountain cults" or "*gzhi bdag* cults" (Blondeau and Steinkellner, 1998: viii).

Attempts, however, have been made to subsume these cults by the Bon religion and Tibetan Buddhism (TB) and to replace "ontic" landscapes

Figure 1.2 A *la btsas* – the *pho brang* of a *gzhi bdag* (a structure demarcating the palace of a *gzhi bdag*)

(Permission from Awang)

(Lightfoot, 1986: 186) with virtual "epistemic" landscapes (Kiely and Jessup, 2016: 124). Epistemic landscapes are characterised by the de-wilding, de-souling, subjugation and re-mapping of nature (McKay, 2013) and are "devoid of ontic substance" (Tacey, 2013: 139), leading, for Animists, to a state of "absolute nonbeing" and "chaos" (Eliade, 1959: 64).

As a result of the "cultural editing of the Tibetan world" (Huber, 1999: 32), enspirited sacred natural sites are often discursively excluded by TB clergy (as a despised mundane tradition) and in addition by *homo ratio* and most conservationists because they are inhabited, owned, managed and governed by other-than-human persons.

Historically the cultural identity of Tibetan nomads and farmers was predicated on the honouring of their regional gods (*yul lha*) and the local *numina* (*gzhi bdag*) that inhabit most montane sacred natural sites.[3] Most mountains in the Tibetan world are inhabited by a *gzhi bdag* associated with specific lay communities and territories (Awang, 2014). They are part of an Animistic and shamanistic tradition concerned with the immediate world, involving various ceremonies and rituals that take place in the home and mountain locales (Studley, 2005).

The *gzhi bdag* and 'gods of the past', mythically subdued by Buddhism and the Bon religion, are closer to Tibetan nomads and farmers in geography, identity and in sensed presence. In the world of the lay Tibetan, many landscape features point back to the worship of ancient spirits. They are not only conscious of the constant scrutiny of *gzhi bdag* when they go hunting, but they also engage in rituals and place demands on them for protection and health, and success, in hunting, trading, travel, farming, etc. Participation in mountain cults is still an essential element of rural Tibetan life, and identity and is expressed in cultural, economic, eco-spiritual and political behaviour. Additionally, as a "spontaneously recovered folk practice" (Schwartz, 1994: 227), the *gzhi bdag* cult lies outside state control and is a contemporary means of expressing unique identity.

The psycho-spiritual behaviour exhibited within the domain of the *gzhi bdag* might be described by conservationists as 'explicit nature conservation'. In reality, however, the behaviour is much more complex and sophisticated, with humankind comprising only one element of the "cosmoscape" (Reichel, 2012: 140). 'Nature conservation' and 'custodianship' are both different from the Indigenous concept of "belonging to nature" (Callicott, 1989: 194).

To maintain equilibrium (or *snod bcud do mnyam* in Tibetan) between the human-bio-physical-spiritual worlds and enjoined by the *gzhi bdag*, local people are obliged to treat animals and plants as "part of a reciprocating matrix of persons" (Oriel, 2014: 50). Tibetans are not attached to and do not identify physically with SNS (Studley, 2012) because they are socially and culturally constructed as places and categories (Verschuuren, 2007). It is not the physical elements of SNS that are important, but the topocosmic inter-relationship renders the resources apparent and concrete (Lye, 2005; Nightingale, 2006).

1.3 The role of Tibetan spirits of place in spiritual governance

The *numina* or *gzhi bdag* that inhabit enspirited SNS in Tibet are not only place owners (*gzhi* = *place*), but as *bdag po*, they hold absolute power and authority as 'Lords' and 'Governors' (Mills, 2003) of the mountain abodes over which they have jurisdiction. Their power extends to their genealogical titles, which suggest a strong sense of spiritual kinship with humankind. Furthermore, they are *de jure/de facto* custodians of all the biophysical resources within their domain and are considered as 'juristic persons' (see section 1.5), in all but name, with anthropomorphic characteristics (Studley, 2005).

Their *modus operandi* of interaction with humankind is predicated on a "legal relationship" (Petrazycki, 2011: 192) of "contractual reciprocity" (Coggins and Hutchinson, 2006: 93) in which humankind does not hold a place of natural authority. The *gzhi bdag* exercise "spiritual governance" (Bellezza, 1997: 41) and provide patronage, blessing and protection on the condition that humankind honours and appeases them regularly and complies with their behavioural expectations in terms of protecting their property (including *flora/fauna*), especially when visiting their abode (Studley, 2014).

Spiritual governance is autochthonous (native) and predicated solely on the agency of *numina* that, as owners, hold absolute power and authority. The *numina* decide on the objectives of governance and their pursuance and orchestrate through intermediaries the decision-making process. The primary objective of spiritual governance by all the participants is predicated on the maintenance of equilibrium among the human, biophysical and spirit worlds. Participants in this case typically include the *numina* (*gzhi bdag*), headmen, villagers, spirit-helpers, trance mediums, divination masters and sometimes Tibetan doctors and Lamas.

1.4 The role of local Tibetan people in the ritual protection of SNS

It is evident from field research (Studley, 2014) in north-western Yunnan that most human beings attempt to interact with *numina* on the basis of contractual reciprocity in return for patronage, governance, protection and blessing. One important aspect of this book is the role of Indigenous and local people in the ritual protection of the domain of a *gzhi bdag* which constitutes an SNS. Significantly, the abode of a *gzhi bdag* is an underground *pho brang* or palace, which is demarcated by a *la btsas* (Figure 1.2). Among Tibetan laymen, local *numina* (*gzhi bdag*) are honoured and appeased through the building of *la btsas*, which are wooden or stone structures on the middle slopes of mountains or hilltops. *La btsas* are annually constructed in ceremonies varying according to the lunar calendar. This is one of the oldest Tibetan customs and is found in all regions inhabited by Tibetans and some Qiangic areas and has continued to the present day without interruption.

Although the taboos and rituals associated with the ritual protection of SNS and its spiritual governance are not necessarily perceived as instruments of resource management, by the people who practise them, they often "have functions similar to those of institutions of formal nature conservation" (Colding and Folke, 2001: 584) and so should not be ignored.

Tibetan lay people often engage in ritual enquiry with the help of a trance medium or divination specialist in response to a vision, trance, omen, theophany or calamity in order to decide if any *numina* are upset with them, and if so which *numina*, what offence has been committed and what types of restitution are required.

Although *gzhi bdag* are autocratic in terms of governance, they are dependent upon the human beings to re-enspirit their domain by engaging in invocation rituals and liturgies. Re-enspiriting should be done at least annually by the community, and *gzhi bdag* should be invoked by name and their terrestrial abode re-designated and re-inscribed geospatially through ritual demarcation (Coggins and Zeren, 2014). If not, the *gzhi bdag* will become displaced and de-territorialised and lose their power, status and authority (Ramble, 2008).

1.5 The status and scale of enspirited SNS and their spiritual governance

The importance of enspirited SNS, especially in the homelands of Indigenous people, should not be ignored on the basis of threats from globalisation and secularisation or of imagined limitations in terms of effectiveness or scale of appropriate cultural norms.

Indigenous people have shown remarkable resilience and aptitude for cultural revitalisation in the face of cultural stress or social change (Wallace, 2013). Animism has not died out, as some have suggested (Tippett, 1973), and it has not been replaced by secularism or humanism.

Furthermore, the communication tools of globalisation have allowed threatened Indigenous people groups to network with each other (e.g., Carlson, 2017), and for 'the commons' to become the new narrative for the 21st century, allowing for the creation of self-organised, non-market, non-government systems for the management and governance of shared resources (Weston and Bollier, 2013).

In terms of scale, spiritual governance of SNS is a characteristic behavioural practice by which many of the world's Indigenous people ritually protect much of the world's biodiversity outside formally protected areas (Lynch and Alcorn, 1993). SNS are globally distributed and when aggregated may constitute 12 million km^2 or at least 8% of the world's land surface (Bhagwat and Palmer, 2009). On the Tibetan Plateau alone, SNS have been estimated to cover 25% of the territory (Buckley, 2007), and locally 30% of Ganzi Prefecture (Shen et al., 2012) and 60% of the Yubeng Valley (Studley, 2014). Furthermore, SNS are nodes in a much larger ecological network and an integral part of the social fabric that permeates the whole landscape or territory. Juristic personhood and spiritual governance are important social-cultural mechanisms that explain the extent of the spiritual dimension in the context of the wider landscape.

1.6 The legal status of enspirited SNS

Although the African Commission on Human and Peoples' Rights (ACHPR) resolved in May 2017 to protect sacred natural sites and territories, no reference was made to their legal status. Most jurisdictions in the world do not grant standing to SNS under the law. As a result, their biocultural integrity is being compromised by modernity, mining, development, mass tourism, assimilation, conservation, urbanisation and forced resettlement. They would be most effective as protected areas (PAs) if they could also be granted standing under the law as well as IUCN designation as protected areas.

In what represents a nascent trend since 2014, sacred rivers, catchments, Indigenous homelands and mountains in New Zealand, India and Colombia, often in their entirety, have been granted juristic personhood by legislatures or courts. This legislation augmented by "the rights of nature" (Cano Pecharroman, 2018: online), a growing international movement, has established a precedent for the legal protection of most threatened landscapes, including enspirited sacred natural sites.

As far as many Indigenous peoples and local communities are concerned, the 'spirits of place', or *numina* that enspirit most SNS, are endowed with certain rights as 'juristic persons', in all but name, and these communities regularly invoke their *numina*, enabling them to engage in 'spiritual governance' (Studley and Awang, 2016; Studley and Horsley, 2018).

The concept of juristic personhood refers generally to a legal subject that is not a human being, but one which society has decided to recognise as a subject of certain rights, protections, privileges, responsibilities and liabilities (Shelton, 2015).

Given that "spiritual governance" (Bellezza, 1997: 41) is one of the *de facto* responsibilities (or privileges) of the *numina* that inhabit most enspirited SNS, legislation that confers personhood on natural spirited entities could recognise the *numina*'s legal status in its own right and as a contractual obligation (between *numina* and the local people).

Most conservation initiatives aimed at the legal protection of the natural environment are undertaken by *Homo sapiens* acting as the plaintiff and beneficiary, according to human-directed norms. This book argues that if enspirited SNS are granted juristic personhood, they gain standing in their own right as plaintiffs expressing inherent cultural rights and norms, and if their biocultural integrity is threatened (by clearcutting, for example), they can seek legal redress in a court of law through a guardian. Furthermore, the burden of proof rests with the party/parties who are threatening the biocultural integrity of the enspirited SNS.

Historically, most European-based legal systems have "denied legal personhood to natural-spiritual entities" (Jonas, 2017, pers. comm., 29 June). That denial is being reversed in the legislation and cases highlighted in this book predicated on two post-anthropocentric approaches.

It will be argued that these two approaches to the natural environment fall under either the rubric of Animism predicated on posthuman themes or ecocentric 'rights of nature' under the aegis of pan(en)theistic themes (Berry, 1988).

The posthuman represents a "qualitative shift in thinking addressing the basic unit of common reference for our species, our polity and our relationship to the other inhabitants of this planet" (Braidotti, 2013: 6).

Animism is the most ancient, geographically widespread and diverse of all belief systems, adhered to today by some 300 million Indigenous people. It is predicated on the assumption that biophysical entities such as mountains, forests and rocks are capable of being enspirited by spirits of place or *numina* (Sponsel, 2007).

A *numen* is a 'spirit of place' or *genius loci* that is present within an object or place (mountain, forest, spring, idol). *Numina* (the plural of numen) were very common in ancient Rome (Mehta-Jones, 2005), and the same concept continues to be widespread among Indigenous people throughout the world.

Ecocentrism, in contrast, is "a philosophy or perspective that places intrinsic value on all living organisms and their natural environment, regardless of their perceived usefulness or importance to human beings" (dictionary.com).[4] It recognises that "human beings have a responsibility towards the ecosphere and moral sentiments that are increasingly expressed in the language of rights" (Washington et al., undated: online).[5] It has been suggested that the Gaia hypothesis has emerged as a popular symbol of ecocentrism primarily because it has come to be associated with the belief that human-kind is not a dominant species and human consciousness is not the only means through which nature should be judged and interpreted (O'Riordan, 1981).

Panentheism ('all is IN God') adds a transcendent dimension to ecocentrism and is predicated on an intrinsic connection between all living things and the physical universe which accord with 'natural laws'. It assumes a bipolar universe with a separate and greater divine reality outside the material world. Panentheism is part of a gnostic mystic experiential tradition that is informed by Plato, Pierre Teilhard de Chardin and Thomas Berry, by which all things are united under the world soul or *anima mundi*. Berry's mystic panentheism provided the inspiration for movements for Earth Jurisprudence, Wild Law and Earth Law, although Berry emphasised the physical universe rather than the Earth (Berry, 1988).

Pantheism is also linked to ecocentrism as well as becoming popular in some conservation circles (Harrison, 2004). Pantheism "arises out of monism" (Thiselton, 2005: 223), where all of reality is one 'substance' (call the substance 'God' or Nature or the Universe) and there are no personal or anthropomorphic Gods.

It is important to recognise that, in most of the recent cases where juristic personhood has been granted to legal subjects, the subjects are typically inhabited by *numina*. It would appear that legal subjects ever since the *Mullick v. Mullick* case in 1925 are only eligible for juristic personhood status after they have been enspirited. There are Gaian 'panentheists' that claim that all the earth is animated (Harding, 2006) and anthropologists (Hallowell, 2002) who claim that only select subjects become enspirited. Most sacred natural sites are typically enspirited by a unique geospecific spirit with a unique personhood predicated on an Animistic tradition that should not be confused or conflated with bipolar panentheism or with monistic pantheism (Harrison, 2004).

Although the legislation on juristic personhood and the 'rights of nature' provides a new legal framework to protect threatened landscape or 'nature', they both have a very disparate conceptual and philosophic foundation. Given that the rationale for the book is the protection of enspirited SNS in the homelands of Indigenous people, it is necessary to identify the most apposite approach, which resonates with the worldview of Indigenous people. For the purpose of analysis, post-anthropocentric approaches are considered more appropriate, and so ecocentric (Mathews, 1995) will be contrasted with posthuman (Clarke and Rossini, 2016) in the context of polycentric law (Grzeszczak and Karolewski, 2012) and polycentric governance (Nagendra and Ostrom, 2012) in the next chapter.

Notes

1 Glastonbury tor has been a ritual sacred natural site (to honour the sun, snake, earth-goddess) since Neolithic times; its modified spiral structure (maze or labyrinth?) is reflected in the spiral petroglyphs found in caves and the hundreds of ammonites unearthed on its summit (Asher, 1979).

2 By Laika ac from UK (Glastonbury Tor) [CC BY-SA 2.0 (https://creative commons.org/licenses/by-sa/2.0)], via Wikimedia Commons.

3 Typically three *gzhi bdag* sites per village (Studley, 2014).

4 Anon, undated, Ecocentrism www.dictionary.com/browse/ecocentric

5 Washington, H., Taylor, B., Kopnina, H., Cryer, P., and Piccolo, J. (n.d.), updated, *Statement of Commitment to Ecocentrism*. www.ecologicalcitizen.net/statement-of-ecocentrism.php

2 Theoretical basis for post-anthropocentric approaches to nature and jurisprudence

At the root of many of the environmental, economic and social crises we face today is an outdated legal system and a fractured worldview (Capra and Mattei, 2015):

> A world-view that drastically separates mind and body, subject and object, culture and nature, thoughts and things, values and facts, spirit afnd matter, human and nonhuman; a worldview that is dualistic, mechanistic, atomistic, anthropocentric, and pathologically hierarchical – a worldview that, in short, erroneously separates humans from, and often unnecessarily elevates humans above, the rest of the fabric of reality, a broken worldview that alienates men and women from the intricate web of patterns and relationships that constitute the very nature of life and Earth and cosmos.
>
> (Wilber, 2001: 12)

Wilber goes on to argue (2001: 4) that

> the only way we can heal the planet, and heal ourselves, is by replacing this fractured worldview with a paradigm that is more holistic, more relational, more integrative, more Earth-honouring, and less arrogantly human-centred. A worldview, in short, that honours the entire web of life, a web that has intrinsic value in and of itself.

A corresponding paradigm shift is also required in jurisprudence and in the public conception of the law. It is now urgently needed, since the major problems of our time are systemic problems, and our global crisis is an ecological crisis in the broadest sense of the term (Capra and Mattei, 2015).

Much of the recent legislation (see Chapters 4 and 5) addressing the legal status of natural entities appears to represent a nascent trend away from the anthropocentric. It has, however, mostly been predicated on either 'rights of nature' or 'juristic personhood', and it is important to understand the conceptual difference between the two and to identify approaches that resonate with the Animistic worldview of Indigenous people who protect most enspirited SNS.

The 'rights of nature' legislation appears to have been mostly articulated under the aegis of "ecocentric themes" (Clarke and Rossini, 2016: 139) and juristic personhood mostly under "posthuman themes" (Vaccari, 2012: 169).

The posthuman themes considered in this book appear to be mostly predicated on Animism and the ecocentric themes mostly on Gaian panentheism. To reiterate, it is important not to confuse the two, especially when both are used in the context of the same legislation (Plurinational State of Bolivia, 2010; *Miglani v State of Uttarakhand and Others*, 2017).

2.1 Ecocentric themes

Ecocentric themes, namely Earth Governance (Cullinan, 2011) and 'rights of nature' (Weston and Bollier, 2013), have proved successful in advancing the legal status of sacred natural sites (ACHPR, 2017) and protecting rivers (Daly, 2012) and seemingly in providing the legal tools to ensure the integrity of protected and conserved areas. They appear to draw mostly on the work of Thomas Berry (1999). The approach, however, does not resonate

Table 2.1 Ecocentric and posthuman continuum

Ecocentric Themes		Posthuman Relational Themes
Universal/monistic	Worldview	Pluriversal/multiple worlds
Pan(en)theism/ mysticism/gaia	Philosophic/ Spiritual base	Animism
Rights of Nature, Wild Law, Earth Jurisprudence	Legal Framework	Juristic Personhood/ polycentric/ commons
Animated landscapes	Sacred Geography	Enspirited landscapes
Natural laws	Norm Auditing	Spiritual governance
Earth-centric	Focus	Web of life
Epistemic	Engagement with Nature	Ontic
Nature-centric ontology	Ontology	Relational ontology (human-nonhuman)
"Enlightened anthropocentrism"[1]	Agency	Other-than-human agency

well with an Animistic worldview or provide a platform for spiritual governance as defined in this book because most ecocentric approaches appear to be underpinned by panentheism or pantheism.

Panentheism, to reiterate, assumes an intrinsic connection between all living things and the physical world and focuses on mystic advancement when all things will merge with the 'world soul' (or *anima mundi*). It assumes a bipolar universe with a separate and greater divine reality outside the material world. This contrasts with the worldview of Indigenous Animists who do not engage in mystic practice or recognise a bipolar universe and engage personally and ontically with mundane spirits.

Pantheism "arises out of monism" (Thiselton, 2005: 223) where all of reality is one 'substance' (call the substance 'God' or Nature or the Universe or whatever you want), and there are no personal or anthropomorphic Gods. Monistic pantheistic robs particular life forms (including *numina*) of their own measure of significance and agency (Plumwood, 2002) and "erases the particularity of place and ecosystem, the diversity of life, the distinctiveness of culture and of ecological life strategies" (Northcott, 1996: 113).

Furthermore, the ecocentric 'rights' approach does not appear to resonate well with the worldview of the local people who protect most enspirited SNS. The concept of 'rights' is a "construction from outside an Indigenous animistic context" (Solon, 2014: 2).

2.2   Posthuman relational themes

The posthuman relational themes that appear superficially to be germane include Juristic Personhood (Studley, 2017b), cosmotheandric spirituality (Panikkar, 1993) and "new Animism" (Harvey, 2005: 3), articulated under the aegis of "new commons" (Hess, 2008: 1) and a pluriversal worldview (Escobar, 2008).

To reiterate, the concept of juristic personhood refers generally to a legal subject that is not a human being, but one which society has decided to recognise as a subject of certain rights, protections, privileges, responsibilities and liabilities (Shelton, 2015). It appears to conceptually resonate with the worldview of Indigenous Animists. Animistic peoples not only recognise other-than-human persons, but they also often have a socially defined legal relationship with the *numina* that inhabit their SNS who they consider as juristic persons, in all but name (see Chapters 4 and 5).

Although cosmotheandric spirituality (Panikkar, 1993) embraces other-than-human persons, it is, nevertheless, a manifestation of panentheism. It merges the natural, the divine and the human by dynamically unifying them in a mystic experience of triadic oneness existing on all levels of consciousness and reality. Attempts have been made to apply cosmotheandric 'reality' in the context of Indigenous people (Hall and Hendricks, 2013) on the basis of a triadic cosmology, their deep "connection to the cosmic rhythms", and their "natural mysticism" (Hall and Hendricks, 2013: 491, 500). The concept of "natural mysticism" was developed by the contemplative mystic Wayne Teasdale (2010: 175) as a means of including Indigenous people under the aegis of "universal spirituality" (2010: 109). His mystic vision is predicated on the conflation of all spiritual traditions leading to unification with nature. There is very little evidence that most Indigenous lay people engage in any form of self-induced mystic states, and it is arguable if shamans or trance mediums are true mystics (Hitchcock and Jones, 1976) or that spirit possession can be equated to a mystical experience (Schmidt and Huskinson, 2010). Furthermore, for most Indigenous people, the world is 'more than human'; they envision "a world where many worlds fit" (Stahler-Sholk, 2000: 1), and any 'connection' between the human-natural-spiritual worlds is predicated on an ontic "lived experience" (Ingold, 2000: 1) or a "lived relationship" (Blanc and Tovey, 2017: 180), which is consistent with Animism rather than mysticism.

It is important not to confuse Indigenous Animism with "new Animism" (Harvey, 2005: 3). So-called new Animism only exhibits partial resonance with the worldview of most of the local people who protect enspirited SNS. The emphasis of new Animism is on knowing how to behave appropriately with other-than-human persons but who "are only alive when participating in a relationship but not as a result of *numina* taking up residence" (Whitehead, 2013: 88). This contrasts with most Animistic societies where enspirited entities remain enspirited and the resident *numina* remain active (in governance) indefinitely, although if they are ignored the *numina* eventually become displaced (Ramble, 2008).

2.2.1   The commons as a posthuman theme

The 'commons' which have recently evolved represent a posthuman trajectory that is significant for the governance of SNS (by *numina*). Conceptually the "posthuman commons" (Nikolic, 2017: 459) have some resonance with the governance of common land in the UK prior to the Acts of Enclosure. The enclosure movement (1645–1882), however, signified a shift in the attitudes of society towards the environment (Illich, 1983). The shift "entailed seeing the environment as a resource to be exploited for human need instead of a common to be cherished, shared and nourished through practices of care" (Singh, 2017: 752).

Resisting this dominant shift, many Indigenous people and others have continued to view the commons as a source of sustenance of life that needs to be nurtured with relations of care predicated on "thinking-feeling with the earth" (Escobar, 2015: 12).

Several authors (Weston and Bollier, 2013; Ostrom, 2015) argue that 'commons' are a socio-cultural phenomenon, and they make a distinction between 'commons', as a form of nurture, governance and protection, and common pool resources as a class of goods, where the exclusion (of outsiders) is difficult and there is a high degree of "subtractability" (Ostrom et al., 1994: 7). Importantly a commons as a posthuman trajectory is a regime for managing and governing common pool resources (Weston and Bollier, 2013).

Furthermore, the 'Commons' has become an increasingly widespread platform to challenge neoliberal forces (Tyżlik-Carver, 2016). The new 'commoners' want to roll back the pervasive privatisation, nationalisation and marketisation of their shared resources and reassert greater participatory care and governance over their 'common-wealth' and community life. Consequently, anthropologists, sociologists, conservationists, Indigenous peoples and local communities have identified a range of local "commons paradigms" (Bollier, 2007: 27) typically under the rubric of the "pluriverse" (Escobar, 2015: 404). Most "ecological commons" (Morrison, 1995: 16) are distinctively local and have their own social norms and institutions. They are "inalienably tied to the land inhabited by a people, and shaped by their cosmological beliefs, spiritual beliefs and other fundamental aspects of their identity" (Hardison, 2006: online).[2]

There is also a nascent trend to include sacred sites as examples of commons, notably "sacred commons" (Rutte, 2011: 2387) or "spiritual commons" (Samakov and Berkes, 2017: 422). As spiritual commons, SNS is meaningful due to the ritual practices that are performed and the relational ontology the local people have with the site, the resident *numina* and the pluriverse (Escobar, 2015).

2.2.2 Pluriversal worldviews

Pluriversal worldviews (James, 1977) appear to resonate with Indigenous worldviews and challenge Western hegemony and universality, a nature-culture dichotomy, monophasic epistemologies, unitary ontologies, monistic pantheism and the "bipolar theism" (Geisler and Watkins, 2003: 107) of panentheism. They create space for the acceptance of multiple worlds, invoking alternative epistemologies (ways of knowing) and ontologies (ways of being) in different worlds (Baksh and Harcourt, 2015). This does not imply any diminished significance of the *anthropos*. Instead, it signals the significance of all the various agencies that together make up the pluriverse, in which humans reside and act. Recognising the proliferation of human and non-human agencies, it admits the possibility not only that "we have never been modern" (Latour, 2012: book title) but the existence of the 'more-than-human world' (Blaser, 2010). The concept of the pluriverse is drawn from and resonates with an Indigenous relational worldview that recognises a "world where many worlds fit" (Stahler-Sholk, 2000: 1). It is being harnessed by Indigenous groups to re-work conservation ideas and practice (de la Cadena, 2010). The pluriversal worldview, significantly, is not leading to a cultural clash with a universal worldview, but it is providing "a certain freedom to modify, appropriate, and reappropriate without being trapped in imitation" (Minh-ha, 2014: 161).

2.3   Polycentric legal frameworks

Of significance for the legal status of enspirited landscapes (and juristic personhood) is the advent of "late modern law" (Allard and Skogvang, 2015: 62). It represents a break from traditional monolithic statutory legal regimes or "statist law" (Sarat and Kearns, 2009: 248) and a renaissance of polycentric systems of law (Grzeszczak and Karolewski, 2012) and governance (Nagendra and Ostrom, 2012), which have provided a theoretical model for cultural and spiritual commons (Hess, 2008).

Polycentric law is a generic term covering multiple legal regimes including statist law, non-state law, private law, *sui generis* norms and customary law (Sheleff, 2013). Polycentric governance is characterised by a network where multiple independent actors (including non-human ones) order their relationships with one another under a general system of rules or norms (Ostrom, 1972), which is a fundamental concept in commons scholarship (Carlisle and Gruby, 2017).

According to Bell (1992: online), the "ubiquity of 'statist' jurisprudence comes in part from the influence of 'legal positivists' and analytic philosophers, who typically view State law as the only kind of law". Polycentric law, in contrast, is predicated on the express consent of those it serves (Sponsel, 2012), and in a broad sense the polycentric legal order is contractual (Fuller, 1969). The adoption of polycentric post-statist governance is particularly evident within the EU (Modéer, 2016) and environmental regulation since the 1980s (Jacobsen, 2016).

Polycentrism offers a much wider interpretation of the law as it emerges out of several legal subjects and is a way of acknowledging a situation in which more than one legal system can be both legal and legitimate (state law, international law, and customary law) rather than competing trajectories of law (Modéer, 2016).

Polycentric law is important for Indigenous people because customary law is often regarded as invalid because judges are unwilling to expand legal sources beyond legal positivism and legal dogma (Modéer, 2016). Furthermore, judges appear to be unwilling to embrace 'ethnojurisprudence', and lawyers lack the skills required to be ethnojurists. The 'ethnojurist' is "an intercultural communicator, a reconciler of values, a fixer, an arranger, an author, a factotum and many other things" (Zion, 1988: 139).

Customary law "develops organically over extended periods of time and blends with the customs, norms, and rituals of those who practice it" (Bell, 1992: online).

In this chapter, the pertinent philosophies which underpin 'rights of nature' and juristic personhood have been reviewed, and it would appear that posthuman relational themes resonate optimally with the Animistic worldview of most of the people who ritually protect enspirited SNS.

In order to understand the form and meaning of another society's institutions and governance regimes, one must relate them to the local cultural context, not to one's own society (Eberhard, 2014). It is important for 'outsiders' – namely, conservation planners, knowledge-brokers and "ethnojurists" (Zion, 1988: 139) – to understand the philosophies and behavioural practices and spiritual ecologies (see Chapter 3) of the local people who ritually protect enspirited SNS in order to secure the full cooperation of all actors (human and non-human) and represent their interests.

Notes

1 Cohen and Tauber (2013: 30)
2 Hardison, 2006, *Indigenous Peoples and the Commons* http://www.onthe commons.org/Indigenous-peoples-and-commons#sthash.wpMY4pIj

3 Indigenous spiritual ecology

The spiritual governance of enspirited SNS by 'juristic persons' most commonly occurs among Indigenous peoples and is usually contingent upon a nexus of up to twelve characteristic traits (Figure 3.1). These include 'Animism', 'shamanism', 'supernatural ownership-mastery of nature', 'non/human personhood', 'kinship relations', 'covenants', 'reciprocity', 'topocosmic equilibrium', 'eco-spiritual auditing', 'relational ontologies' and 'non/human agency', which singly and collectively result in the generation of 'sui generis norms' or customary laws.

3.1 Animism

To reiterate from Chapter 1, Animism is the most ancient, geographically widespread and diverse of all belief systems, adhered to today by some 300 million Indigenous people (Sponsel, 2012), and 1.266 billion if Indian Hindus are included (Tiwari, 2002). Contrary to popular belief, Animism is not dying out (Tippett, 1973), and it has not been replaced by secularism or humanism. Indeed, at least 40% of the world's population are Animists (van Rheenen, 2013), and the growth of Animism is described as a trend of the future (Myers, 1994). It is predicated on the assumption that biophysical entities such as mountains, forests and rocks are capable of being inhabited by *numina* (Sponsel, 2007). For an Animist, one aspect of some (but not all) natural resources actually is the deity, in contrast to other traditions where they only may represent the deity or its divine aspects (Seeland, 1993).

It is important at this juncture to differentiate between 'sacred' and 'enspirited' and 'animate' and 'live' from an Indigenous and legal perspective. Several examples highlight this distinction.

In the 1930s the anthropologist Irving Hallowell asked an old Ojibwa man if "all the stones we see about us here are 'alive'". The man reflected for a long while and then replied "No! But some are" (Hallowell, 2002: 24). Hallowell asked this question because in Ojibwa and other Algonquian languages, rocks are grammatically 'animate' rather than grammatically

Figure 3.1 Indigenous traits that coalesce around spiritual governance

'inanimate' (Harvey, 2005). Although most biophysical entities are capable of being enspirited, it seemingly requires human agency to 'call down' (Bellezza, 2005) deities to enspirit them. If regular (bi-annual) re-enspiriting is neglected, eventually the *numina* becomes displaced and seeks embodiment elsewhere (Ramble, 2008), and the entity returns to its natural state.

Among the Qiang people, all white quartz rocks are 'sacred' because historically they provided guiding markers on their migration route to the Upper Min Jiang river catchment (southwest China). Although all such rocks are 'sacred', only certain rocks are enspirited as a result of human agency. The Qiang enspirit the five white rocks they place on the roofs of their houses and re-enspirit them on a regular basis. On the third day of the first lunar month, each household honours and appeases the *numina* that inhabit each rock, on their roof (Figure 3.2), in order to secure protection and blessing.

In India, judges do not recognise that an idol or temple is a 'juristic person' (see Chapter 4) until the idol or temple has been enspirited in a *pran pratishtha* ceremony (Mukherjea and Sen, 2013).

Figure 3.2 An enspirited white stone on a Qiang house in Taoping, China
(Studley, photo taken in 2013)

3.2   Shamanism

There is no single agreed-upon definition for the word 'shamanism' among anthropologists (Wikipedia)[1], and perhaps for the purpose of this book, trance medium or even divination practitioner might be more apposite. A trance medium (in common with a shaman) is someone who has access to the "world of spirits" (Romain, 2009: 39). They typically enter into a trance state during a ritual and may practice divination and healing and operate as a channel for communication. Trance mediums (Figure 3.3) play an important role in Animistic societies by helping to maintain equilibrium within the "cosmos-cape" (Reichel, 2012: 140) and for determining the best means of making restitution if local *numina* are upset.

There are many examples of the role of 'shaman' in mediating in Indigenous societies. For example, the Naxi people of Yunnan Province (China) make offerings to a *numen* named *shu*, usually at a spring or pond, mediated through a *Dongba* as a way of compensating for the non-timber forest products collected from the woods and as a means of reconciliation with nature. This ensures not only that they live in harmony with the spirit world but also that they receive environmental and social 'blessing' (Kelkar et al., 2003).

3.3   Spiritual owners-masters of land and flora and fauna

Many Indigenous societies appear to be presided over by spiritual owners-masters of territory, nature, animals or plants and corresponding to what Hultkrantz (1961: book title) terms "the supernatural owners of nature".

The *modus operandi* of the owner-masters is predicated on contractual reciprocity in that they control and protect as well as being responsible for

Figure 3.3 A Mosuo Daba preparing to go into a trance
(Studley, photo taken in 2004)

well-being, providing they are honoured and appeased. Fausto (2008) argues that an understanding of (spiritual) control and mastery are as central to understanding Indigenous socio-cosmologies as affinity (i.e., kinship relationships).

Examples are found in the Amazon (Fausto, 2008) among the Arawete (de Castro, 1992) and the Mapuche-Huilliche (Lausche and Burhenne-Guilmin, 2011).

3.4   Personhood

The western concept of personhood appears to contrast with that of Indigenous cultures that often exhibit "bonds of affection" (Seeland, 1993: 356–358) towards all the elements of the cosmoscape and regard them all as 'persons'. For Indigenous peoples,

> "persons" are not a small select group of rational-minded individuals, rather personhood is ascribed to a vast range of diverse phenomena. Humans are not in a position to demarcate personhood, for they are just one element of a matrix of reciprocating persons.
>
> (Oriel, 2014: online)[2]

Examples of spirit persons are found among the Ojiba (Hallowell, 1960) and the Mapuche (Bacigalupo, 2010).

3.5   Kinship

Supernatural persons may be powerful and operate on the basis of contractual reciprocity with humankind, but they are nevertheless members of the same 'kincentric' community in which humans and non-humans are viewed as part of an inter-relational assemblage which is regarded as an extended family (Salmon, 2000). Kinship relations predicated on sharing and relating to (non/human persons) are commonplace among Indigenous peoples.

Examples include the Batek (Turnbull, 1976), the Mbuti (Turnbull, 1976), the Nayaka (Bird-David, 1999) and the Ojibwa (Hallowell, 2002).

Figure 3.4 Totem poles are a visual representation of kinship and of covenants between humans and other-than-humans

(Creative Commons, Ron Clausen, CC-BY-SA 4.0)[3]

3.6   Covenants (of reciprocity or ritual exchange)

Under the rubric of 'personhood' and 'kinship', there is also evidence of consensual contracts, covenants, legal relationships or agreements between Indigenous societies and local spirit 'owners' or 'masters'.

Examples include the Magars (De Sales, 2011) and the Miskitu (Jamieson, 2009).

Contracts are often observed in clan names and 'totems' (Deloria, 1999) and are mediated under the aegis of shamanistic cultures (De Sales, 2001).

Covenants or pacts also exist between Indigenous people and land, animals, fish and plants (Deloria, 1999; Landerer, 2009; Martin, 1982).

There is evidence that broken covenants are being atoned for (Figure 3.5) between humankind and other-than-human persons, namely with the salmon 'people' (Couch, 2010) and the buffalo 'people' (The American Bison Society, 2016; Leroy Little Bear, 2016, pers. comm., 26 Nov).

3.7   Reciprocity

Reciprocity is defined as non-monetised giving and receiving and is commonly practised in Indigenous societies. It enables Indigenous people to maintain equilibrium and "mutual nurturance" (Whitt, 2009: 54) among the natural, human and spiritual domains (Studley, 2010). It has

Figure 3.5 Atonement for a broken covenant between the Winnemem Wintu and the salmon people

(Photo by Marc Dadigan – used with permission)

long been recognised that "cosmic cycles of reciprocity" (Studley, 2012: 227) are fundamental to ethno-economies with a more-than-human worldview.

Examples are found among the Quechuan (Nuccetelli et al., 2013), the Anishinaabe (Davidson-Hunt and Berkes, 2003), the Mapuche (Ngenpin, n.d.), the Kluane (Nadasdy, 2005) and the Jharkhand *adivasi* (Parajuli, 1999).

3.8 Equilibrium

Equilibrium is defined as the customary ritual nurturance of harmony, balance and good relations among all the elements (human, natural and spiritual) of the cosmos (Studley, 2014; Trask, 2007).

Examples are found among many Indigenous people (Pungetti et al., 2012), including the Ubutu (Chuwa, 2014), the Magar (De Sales, 2011) and the Tuvans (Hou, 2016).

3.9 Auditing

Eco-spiritual auditing is an Indigenous "double monitoring system to cross-check and assess local and regional eco-spiritual conditions which are also tracked in the contexts of a grander eco-cosmic whole as the landscape is part of the cosmoscape" (Reichel, 2012: 140). Furthermore, typically the position of each community is negotiated through material and spiritual dynamics to periodically maintain the ethno-eco-cosmic linkages (Wright, 2013).

Eco-spiritual auditing is typically practised in 'polyphasic' cultures and is characterised by "engaging multiple senses" (Day, 2013: 45) – namely, the physical senses (sight, smell, sound, taste, touch) and intuition, spiritual sense and body sense. The spiritual senses are particularly important among Indigenous people (as well as in mainstream faiths). Modern anthropologists have been cataloguing the spiritual abilities of Indigenous peoples for the last century, confirming they are still "in command of many *spiritual senses* lost to civilized humanity" (Missett, 2008: 17). The spiritual senses typically embrace dreams, visions, omens, trances and theophanies.

Shaman/trance mediums typically play an important role in auditing health (human, plant and livestock) and the biosphere in order to maintain equilibrium within the cosmoscape.

Examples are found in the Mamberamo-Foja region of PNG (Shen et al., 2015), the Amazon (Reichel, 1992) and the peoples of Lugu Lake (Studley, 2004).

3.10 Relational ontologies

The life-ways of many Indigenous people is predicated on maintaining relationships with *numina* typically mediated by 'shaman' or trance mediums. The relationship with *numina* is dependent upon differing sets of "relational ontologies" (Ingold, 2006: 9) and "relational epistemologies" (Bird-David, 1999: S67), which are expressed through the living experience of place-specific rituals (Insoll, 2011). The rituals help to maintain contractual reciprocity and ensure equilibrium and prevent retribution. The *numina* agree to provide patronage, protection and blessing on the condition that humankind honour, thank, appease and invoke them, make restitution with, behave correctly in their domain, protect their property and engage in ritual enquiry to understand their demands.

Examples are found among the Tserangding-pa (Yeh, 2016, pers. comm., 6 Oct), the Lahu (Walker, 2011), the Maya (Montejo, 2008) and the Objiwa (Hallowell, 2002).

3.11 Agency

Agency is the capacity of an 'actor' to act in any given environment or social structure. Among most Indigenous peoples, a range of other-than-human actors exhibit agency in both shaping their environment and making choices individually and collectively (Miller and Davidson-Hunt, 2010).

Examples of spiritual agency are found among many Animists (Watts, 2013), the Sibundoy (McDowell, 2015), the Pikangkun (Hallowell, 1992) and the Mbuti (Turnbull, 1976).

3.12 *Sui generis* norms

Among most Indigenous people, the spiritual governance of SNS is predicated on *sui generis* norms that are 'one of a kind' and enjoined by a spirit in contrast to statist laws, which are predicated on human agency and formally codified. In the context of spiritual governance, *sui generis* norms are often referred to as 'taboos', by anthropologists, from the Polynesian (*tabu*) or Māori (*tapu*). In general, *tapu* expresses the "process of setting a . . . location aside to serve as a ritually protected space" (Issitt and Main, 2014: 454). Taboos are invisible examples of informal institutions, where "norms, rather than governmental juridicial laws and rules, guide human behaviour and conduct toward the natural environment" (Colding and Folke, 2001: 584).

Examples include Indian sacred groves (Gadgil and Vartak, 1976), Kuna spirit sanctuaries (Chapin, 1991), the *ala faly* forests of Southern Madagascar (Tengö et al., 2007) and the domains of Naxi nature spirits (He Hong et al., 2010).

An understanding of the traits that underpin Indigenous spiritual ecology, reviewedherein, provide a platform to examine (in the next chapters) the concepts of juristic personhood and spiritual governance and their legal basis.

Notes

1 Anon, undated, Shamanism http://shamanjon.com/about-shamanism/definition-of-shamanism/
2 Oriel, E. (2014), Whom Would Animals Designate as "Persons"? On Avoiding Anthropocentrism and Including Others, *Journal of Evolution and Technology* 24(3). https://jetpress.org/v24.3/Oriel.htm
3 By Ron Clausen (own work) https://creativecommons.org/licenses/by-sa/4.0

4 Legal background to juristic personhood

Juristic personhood has a pedigree which goes back to Roman law, but it was limited initially to the legal personhood of organisations of people and a variety of collegial institutions. In terms of its present application, both the ancient laws of *jus gentium* and 'public trusts' have provided important staging posts (Shelton, 2015).

4.1 The doctrine of public trusts

The ancient laws of *jus gentium*, which later developed into the 'public trust' doctrine, were formulated by the Byzantine Emperor Justinian (Sandars, 1917), who held that the sea, the shores of the sea, the air and running water were common to everyone. This principle became the law in England, which distinguishes between private property capable of being owned by individuals and certain common resources that the monarch holds in inalienable trust for present and future generations. Many common law courts have adopted and applied public trust law (Shelton, 2015). These laws confer trusteeship or guardianship on the government, with an initial focus on fishing rights and access to the shore, navigable waters and the lands beneath them. After the publication of an influential law review article by Joseph Sax (1970), courts in the United States began to expand the doctrine of public trusts and apply it to other resources, including wildlife and public lands (e.g., *Wade v. Kramer*, 1984). This is included in the constitutions of Pennsylvania, Hawaii, Rhode Island and Alaska (Shelton, 2015).

Public trusts, however, like corporations, are normally constituted only for the benefit of human beings. A more far-reaching measure is required to confer juristic personhood and direct rights on other-than-human persons (Hallowell, 2002). Various attempts have been made in modern times to accord legal status to other-than-human persons.

4.2 Granting legal status to non-human persons

In 1925 colonial judges in India conferred juristic personhood on temples, idols (Figure 4.1) and deities (*Mullick v. Mullick*, 1925) contingent upon the enspiriting of an idol and Salmond's definition of "person" (1913: 18). Importantly, an idol does not develop into a juristic person until it is enspirited (Figure 4.2) during a *Pran Pratistha* ceremony (Mukherjea and Sen, 2013). Salmond defined "person" (1913: 82) in the following way:

> So far as legal theory is concerned, a person is any being whom the law regards as capable of "rights and duties". Any being that is so capable is a person, whether a human being or not, and no being that is not so capable is a person even though he be a man.

Figure 4.1 An idol of Radha Shyamsunderji (similar to the one above) was recognised as a 'juristic person' in 1925 (*Mullick v. Mullick*)

(Permission from Rrahul Yadav www.yadavhistory.com)

Figure 4.2 An idol of Krishna and Radha being enspirited at a *pran pratisha* ceremony

(Permission from V.S. Dasa https://iskcondesiretree.com/)

In a seminal article, 'Should Trees Have Standing?', Stone (1972) argued that the granting of legal personality should not be limited to corporations and ships but should include animals,[1] trees, rivers and the environment. Stone's innovation was to propose that the interests of nature should be represented by a guardian and that the burden of proof should rest upon the party that had allegedly compromised the integrity of the ecosystem or organism. Stone's comments echoed remarks made by US Supreme Court Justice William O. Douglas, who in a dissenting opinion argued in a landmark environmental law case (*Sierra Club v. Morton*, 1972) that environmental objects should have standing to sue in court.

In the years since Stone's and Douglas's comments, various innovations in law (outlinedas follows) have allowed for 'nature rights' to be recognised in Ecuador and Bolivia, 'juristic personhood' to be granted to biophysical entities in New Zealand, India and Colombia, and for SNS to be recognised in Africa.

4.3   Legal status for Mother Earth

In 2008, Ecuador became the first country in the world to declare in its constitution that 'nature', or Pachamama, is a legal entity. Pachamama is the name of an earth-goddess (mother goddess), who is a *huaca* or *numina* who may adopt the *persona* of the Virgin Mary (Derks, 2009). Articles 10 and 71–74 of the Constitution (Ecuador National Assembly, 2008) recognise the inalienable rights of ecosystems, give individuals the authority to petition on behalf of ecosystems and require the government to remedy violations of Pachamama (Figure 4.3) or nature's rights. It states that:

> Nature or Pacha Mama has the right to exist, persist, maintain and regenerate its vital cycles, structure, functions and its processes in evolution.
>
> (Article 71)

On 21 May 2009, Indigenous churches issued a joint declaration at the UN Permanent Forum on Indigenous Issues recommending that the forum recognise Mother Earth as a legal subject (WCC, 2009).

Bolivia followed Ecuador's example by similarly amending its constitution to give protection to natural ecosystems (Plurinational State of Bolivia, 2010). The amendments redefined the country's mineral deposits as 'blessings' and established new 'rights for nature', namely:

> the right to life and to exist; the right to continue vital cycles and processes free from human alteration; the right to pure water and clean air; the right to ecological balance; the right to the effective and opportune restoration of life systems affected by direct or indirect human

activities, and the right for preservation of Mother Earth and any of its components with regards to toxic and radioactive waste generated by human activities.

(Article 7)

Figure 4.3 Ecuador granted rights to nature/Pachamama in 2008

(Permission from Jassy Watson (artist) www.earthcirclestudios.com & www.jassy.com.au)

Furthermore, the government appointed an ombudsman to defend or represent Mother Earth.

The constitutional changes made by Bolivia and Ecuador both resulted from and have given new momentum to a "Pachamama movement" (Weston and Bollier, 2013: 60) that has spread to sub-Saharan Africa, Australia, Canada, India, Nepal, New Zealand, the United Kingdom and the United States. It has had a deep influence on 'Harmony with Nature' resolutions in the United Nations General Assembly (2009, 2015, 2016a, 2016b). Efforts have also been made to secure a Universal Declaration of the Rights of Mother Earth at the UN, but these have not been forthcoming to date.

4.4   Granting recognition to sacred natural sites

In 2015 the African Biodiversity Network (ABN) and Gaia Foundation submitted "a call for legal recognition of SNS and territories and their customary governance systems" (ABN, 2016) to the African Commission on Human and Peoples' Rights (ACHPR) predicated on 'earth law' under the aegis of Gaian panentheism (Berry, 1999). In May 2017 the ACHPR resolved to "protect Sacred Natural Sites and Territories" (Clause 44 (iv)).

Note

1 On 4 July 2018, the High Court of Uttarakhand granted juristic personhood to all animals and asked the citizens of Uttarakhand to act as persons *in loco parentis* on behalf of animals (TOI 5/7/2018).

5 Legislative chronology of cases

Although Stone and Douglas first suggested the foundations for ecosystems to become juristic persons in the USA, other nations translated rhetoric into praxis, by introducing legislation that granted legal personhood for ecosystems. Eight examples are summarised in this chapter, and each case is assessed on the nature of the legislation or adjudication, the 'guardianship' measures and the spiritual dimension that is involved.

5.1 Te Urewera, New Zealand

In 2014 New Zealand was the first nation on earth to give up formal ownership of a National Park under the aegis of the *Te Urewera Act* (TNZPCC, 2014) and declare the area known by the local *Tuhoe* as *Te Urewera* (Figure 5.1), a legal person with "all the rights, powers, duties and liabilities of a legal person" (Clause 14(1)). Personhood means that lawsuits to protect the land (*Te Urewera*) can be brought on behalf of the land itself, obviating the need to show harm to a human being.

***

The new legal entity is now administered by the *Te Urewera* Board, which comprises joint *Tuhoe* and Crown membership who are empowered to file lawsuits on behalf of *Te Urewera*. They are mandated:

> to act on behalf of, and in the name of, Te Urewera [and] to provide governance for Te Urewera.
>
> (Schedule 6 Part 2 clauses 17a and 17b)

They may also grant activity permits for:

> the taking, cutting or destroying Indigenous plants within Te Urewera.
>
> (Schedule 3 Clause 1 (1a))

Figure 5.1 Te Urewera, the homelands of the Tuhoe people, declared a legal person in 2014

disturbing, trapping, taking, hunting, or killing Indigenous animals within Te Urewera.

(Schedule 3 Clause 1 (1b))

providing:

the preservation of the species concerned is not adversely affected.
(Schedule 3 Clause 1 (2a))

the effects on Te Urewera are no more than minor.
(Schedule 3 Clause 1 (2b))

the grant of a permit is consistent with the management plan.
(Schedule 3 Clause 1 (2c))

the proposed activity is important for the restoration or maintenance of customary practices that are relevant to the relationship of iwi and hapū to Te Urewera.

(Schedule 3 Clause 1 (3b))

iwi and *hapu* support the application.

(Schedule 3 Clause 1 (3e))

***

   Tuhoe spirituality is directly provided for in Board decision-making, whereby in performing its functions, the Board may consider and give expression to *Tuhoe tanga* (Tuhoe identity and culture) and the Tuhoe concepts that underpin nurturance, namely: *mana* (authority, identity), *mauri* (life force), *kaitiaki* (spiritual guardians), *tikanga* (traditional custom), *ture* (societal guidelines), *tohu* (signs and signals), *tapu* (sacredness), *muru* (social deterrent) and *rahui* (temporary bans).

5.2   Mount Mauna Kea, Hawaii

In a contested court case (*Hou v. BLNR*, 2015, 2016), the descendants of the *Kanaka Maoli* (Native Hawaiians) objected to the installation of a large telescope near the summit of Mount *Mauna Kea* (Figure 5.2) because it is the home of *Mo'oinanea*, a female tutelary spirit. They petitioned for standing for *Mo'oinanea* (Flores, 2011), but the court under Hawaiian law would not grant standing but was willing for her to be represented and to accept the testimony of an expert witness who is a spirit medium (*KAHEA v. UHH*, 2013).

Figure 5.2 Mount Mauna Kea, Hawaii
(Creative Commons, SABO123, 1971, CC-BY-SA 3.0)[2]

The representative wrote an affidavit (accepted by the court) that granted him power of attorney to act and speak on behalf of *Mo'oinanea*. The medium and the representative argued that the mountain summit is an important portal for communicating with *Mo'oinanea* and the *Akua* (ancestral spirits). They reiterated that *Mo'oinanea* had told them in "prayerful mediumship" (Rios, 2016: 2) that if the telescope was built, then access to her and the *Akua* would be severed permanently, and they would no longer receive spiritual guidance. Furthermore, it would result in an imbalance between humans, the spirit world and the environment. The courts decided in favour of the Native Hawaiians because of "lack of due process" (*Hou v. BLNR*, 2015: 2), and they dismissed the appeal due to "lack of appellate jurisdiction" (*Hou v. BLNR*, 2016: 1).

5.3   Te Awa Tupua (Whanganui River), New Zealand

On 15 March 2017, the New Zealand House of Representatives passed the *Te Awa Tupua* (Whanganui River Claims Settlement) Bill (TNZPCC, 2016), declaring that the Whanganui River (Figure 5.3) was a legal person after 170 years of litigation from the Māori. The legislation established a new legal framework for the Whanganui River (or *Te Awa Tupua*), whereby "Te Awa Tupua is a legal person and has all the rights, powers, duties and liabilities of a legal person" (Clause 14 (1)), predicated on a set of overarching 'intrinsic values', or *Tupua te Kawa*.

***

Figure 5.3 Whanganui River declared a juristic person in 2017

(Permission from Geoff Cloake, geoffcloake.co.nz)

The legislation makes provision for two *Te Pou Tupua*, or guardians, appointed jointly from nominations made by *iwi* (Māori confederation of tribes) with interests in the Whanganui River and the Crown. Their role is to "act and speak on behalf of the Te Awa Tupua . . . and protect the health and well-being of the river" (Clause 19 a and b). The *Te Pou Tupua* is 'supported' by a *Te Karewao*, or advisory committee, comprising representatives of Whanganui *iwi*, other *iwi* with interests in the River and local authorities. The *Te Pou Tupua* enter into relationships with relevant agencies, local government and the *iwi* and *hapu* of the river.

***

Furthermore in a 'statement of significance' (schedule 8), recognition is also given to the *numina* or *kaitiaki* that inhabit each of the 240-plus rapids (*ripo*) on the Whanganui River and are each associated with a distinct *hapu* (sub-tribe) given that:

> The kaitiaki provide insight, guidance, and premonition in relation to matters affecting the Whanganui River, its resources and life in general and the hapu invoke (karakia) the kaitiaki for guidance in times of joy, despair, or uncertainty for the guidance and insight they can provide.
>
> (Schedule 8 (3))

5.4   The Ganges River, India

On 20 March 2017, the High Court of Uttarakhand (*Salim v. State of Uttarakhand and Others*, 2017) declared that the:

> Ganga River and all its (115) tributaries and streams . . . are juristic persons with all the corresponding rights duties and liabilities of a living person.
>
> (Clause 19)

***

The court appointed three officials to act as legal custodians responsible for conserving and protecting the rivers and their tributaries and ordered a management board be established within three months.

***

The court's decision was necessary because both rivers are "losing their very existence" (Clause 10) and both "are sacred and revered and presided over by goddesses" (Clause 11).

Figure 5.4 The Ganges River was declared as multiple juristic persons in 2017
(Permission from Richard Haley www.himalayamasala.com/)

5.5 Uttarakhand Himalaya, India

On 30 March 2017, the High Court of Uttarakhand re-examined a previous (failed) petition (*Miglani v. State of Uttarakhand and Others*, 2017) and declared that:

> We, by invoking our 'parens patriae' jurisdiction, declare glaciers including Gangotri & Yamunotri, rivers, streams, rivulets, lakes, air, meadows, dales, jungles, forests wetlands, grasslands, springs and waterfalls, legal entity/legal person/juristic person/juridicial person/ moral person/artificial person having the status of a legal person, with all corresponding rights, duties and liabilities of a living person, in order to preserve and conserve them. They are also accorded the rights akin to fundamental rights/legal rights.
>
> (Clause 2)

***

In contrast to the earlier judgement, the court recognised the role of other riparian states (under the aegis of an inter-state council), community participation and the importance of extending juristic personhood to the Himalayan ecosystem (Figure 5.5). It appointed six government officials to act as persons in *loco parentis* of the geographic features in the State of Uttarakhand and permitted the co-option of seven local representatives.

***

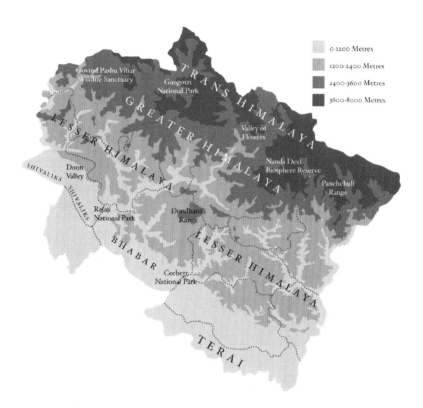

Figure 5.5 The Uttarakhand Himalaya was declared as multiple juristic persons in 2017

(Permission from Rajiv Rawat, ©1997–2010, http://uttarakhand.org)

The judgement quotes repeatedly from *Secret Abode of Fireflies* (Singh, 2009), which underlines the sacredness of mountains (as the abode of deities) and of certain Indian trees and plants, and devotes a chapter to the 'rights of nature'.

On 7 July 2017, in an apparent setback, the Supreme Court of India (*State of Uttarakhand v. Salim*, 2017) 'stayed' the landmark judgement of 20 March (*Salim v. State of Uttarakhand and Others*, 2017) that granted juristic personhood to the Ganga and Yumana Rivers (and their tributaries). The stay resulted not from a challenge to juristic personhood, which was accepted by the Supreme Court, but as a result of ambiguity regarding accountability for damage done to the rivers (*Times of India*, 2017).

5.6 The Atrato River, Colombia

On 2 May 2017, it was publically announced in the national newspaper of Columbia, *El Tiempo*, that the constitutional court had declared the Atrato River Basin a 'subject of rights' meriting special constitutional protection (ABColombia, 2017). The court called on the state to protect and revive the river and its tributaries and the Choco. The state was given six months to eradicate illegal mining and to begin to decontaminate the river and reforest areas affected by illegal mining (some 44,000 ha).

***

The Court also ordered the national government to exercise legal guardianship and representation of the rights of the river (through an institution designated by the President of the Republic), together with the Indigenous ethnic communities (mostly Emberas) that live in the Atrato River Basin in Chocó.

***

Hopefully, the legislation may allow the Emberas to secure standing and protection for some of their *jaikatuma* (Figure 5.6) or spirit mountains (Juducia y Pas, 2009) and defend their Sitios Sagrados Naturales or SNS (OIA, undated; CRIC, undated).

Figure 5.6 Mount Careperro, a sacred spirit mountain
(Permission from Carlos Otalvaro, http://elretornoproducciones.com/)

5.7   Grizzly Bear Spirit valley or Qat'muk, Canada

On 1 November 2017, the Supreme Court of Canada approved, by a majority, a four-season ski resort in Qat'muk (Figure 5.7) and ruled that the Ktunaxa's constitutional right to freedom of religion was not being violated (*Ktunaxa Nation v. BC*, 2017). The decision stems from a lawsuit filed by the Ktunaxa nation after developer Jumbo Glacier Resorts Ltd. received B.C. government approval to proceed. The Ktunaxa consider the land at the foot of Jumbo Mountain (Qat'muk) to be a sacred natural site and say construction of a resort would drive away Grizzly Bear Spirit, a principal figure in their religion.

The Ktunaxa Nation had argued that charter[3] protection for freedom of religion must include not only spiritual beliefs but also underlying sacred sites.

In spite of the dissenting views of Justices Moldaver and Cote, the Supreme Court ruled (by a majority) that religious protections under the charter do not extend that far and only cover freedom to hold such beliefs and the right to manifest them through worship and teaching.

> In short, the charter protects the freedom to worship but does not protect the spiritual focal point of worship.
>
> (*Ktunaxa Nation v. BC*, 2017: Clause 71)

Figure 5.7 Grizzly Bear Spirit valley or Qat'muk, Canada
(Photo courtesy of Robyn Duncan, https://wildsight.ca/)

5.8 Mount Taranaki, New Zealand

On 20 Dec 2017, eight Māori tribes[4] signed a 'record of understanding' (ROU) with the New Zealand government (NIT and The Crown, 2017) to ensure the status of Mount Taranaki (Figure 5.8) as a juristic person in common with *Te Urewera* and *Te Awa Tupua*. The new status of the mountain means if its bio-cultural integrity is threatened, not only does it pose a threat to the *iwi* but the mountain has standing as a plaintiff to seek redress in a court of law.

The ROU also signalled there would be an apology from the Crown and acknowledgement of the historical breaches as a result of the Treaty of Wait-angi (1840).

Furthermore, the Crown and the *Ngāti Maru ki Taranaki* also signed an Agreement in Principle, paving the way for a Deed of Settlement, which will bring Treaty settlements for the Taranaki region to a conclusion.

****

The eight local Māori tribes and the government will share guardian-ship of the sacred mountain on the west coast of the North Island, in a long-awaited acknowledgement of the Indigenous people's relationship to the mountain, who view it as an ancestor (*tupuna*) and a family member (*whanau*).

***

Figure 5.8 Mount Taranaki
Permission from Fiona Clark www.taranakivista.co.nz

Mount Taranaki is *tapu* (sacred) with *mauri* (life force) and is furthermore a *tupuna* (ancestor) who is named *Rua Taranaki*. The Taranaki *iwi* have a "lived relationship" (Blanc and Tovey, 2017: 180) with Mount Taranaki, which traditionally was as a place of pilgrimage, a place for ceremonies, a burial ground, and its forested slopes were an area on which to take flora and fauna which are regarded as *taonga* or treasures (Wilmshurst et al., 2004). It is unknown if the restoration of customary lore and practices will be allowed under the Deed of Settlement in common with Schedule 3 of the Te Urewera Act (2014).

Traditional Māori *tikanga* (custom) dictate that the *tapu* and *mauri* of the mountain must be respected with humans responsible for the "spiritual guardianship" (Lyver and Moller, 2010: 241) or *kaitiaki* of the surrounding environment. To be a *kaitiaki* means looking after one's own blood and bones – literally. One's *whanaunga* (family relations) and *tupuna* (ancestors) include the mountains, plants and animals, rocks and trees, with a custom predicated on sustainable use. The Māori are expected to relate to mountains in a meaningful way because their worldview positions humans as *tangata whenua* (people of the land) and, as such, not above nature but an integral part of it. Under the aegis of Māori lore, the taking of flora and fauna is allowed with some restrictions (*rahui*) to certain areas and times of year. *Karakia* (prayer or incantations) are said before taking any flora and fauna to protect the person, to thank the gods or *atua* for the provision of the resource and to acknowledge the life force (*mauri*) of the resource. If incantation rituals are not performed, it is believed that the *tapu* will be breached and the gods will cause harm to befall the person, including his or her wider family, to the extent of illness and, if the breach is severe, death. Loss of *mana* (authority) would certainly be forthcoming. The custom thus guarantees sustainable use through respect for the world order.

Notes

1 I, Brucieb [GFDL (www.gnu.org/copyleft/fdl.html), CC-BY-SA-3.0 (http://creativecommons.org/licenses/by-sa/3.0/) or CC BY 2.5.
2 By SABO123 (Own work) [CC BY-SA 3.0 (https://creativecommons.org/licenses/by-sa/3.0)], via Wikimedia Commons.
3 Canadian Charter of Rights and Freedoms.
4 Ngāruahine, Taranaki Iwi, Te Atiawa, Ngāti Mutunga, Ngāti Ruanui, Ngaa Rauru Kiitahi, Ngāti Tama, and Ngāti Maru.

6   Litigation to date

Since the mid-1970s, lawyers in the USA have been filing lawsuits in the name of non-humans that involve ecosystems but with only limited success (Stone, 2010). Early named plaintiffs included the Byram River (New York and Connecticut),[1] No Bottom marsh (Somers, NY),[2] Brown brook (Somers, NY),[3] Makena beach (Maui County, Hawaii),[4] Death Valley National Park (California and Nevada),[5] Billerica town common (Massachusetts),[6] some pine trees in Pacific Palisades (LA)[7] and the Palila (Figure 6.1) or *Psittirostra* (or *Loxioides*) *bailleui*, an endangered Hawaiian bird,[8] found only on the upper slopes of Mount Mauna Kea.[9]

There is evidence that the post-2008 constitutional and legal provisions (referred to in Chapter 5) are beginning to give rise to litigation and enforcement based on the legal personhood of nature in Ecuador, the USA and India, but there is a need for judicial traction for 'rights of nature' and juristic personhood to become normative in most jurisdictions.

6.1   Ecuador

The first lawsuit (*Wheeler v. DPGEL*, 2011) was filed on 30 March 2011 against the local government near Rio Vilcabamba, which was responsible for a road expansion project that dumped debris into the river, narrowing its width and thereby doubling its speed. The project was also done without the completion of an environmental impact assessment or consent of the local residents. The case was filed by two residents, citing the violation of the rights of nature, rather than property rights, by the damage done to the river. The case was especially important because the court stated that the rights of nature would prevail over other constitutional rights if they were in conflict with each other, setting an important precedent. The proceedings also confirmed that the burden of proof to show there is no damage lies with the defendant. Though the plaintiffs were granted a victory in court, the enforcement of the ruling has been lacking, as the local government has been slow to comply with the mandated reparations (Daly, 2012).

Figure 6.1 A Palila on the upper slopes of Mauna Kea

(By Photographer Jack Jeffrey, USGS [Public domain], via Wikimedia Commons – https://commons.wikimedia.org/wiki/File:Loxioides_bailleui.jpg)

In a second case (*REANCBRN, 2011*) on 15 June 2011, the government of Ecuador filed a case against illegal gold mining operations in northern Ecuador in the remote districts of San Lorenzo and Eloy Alfaro. The prosecution argued that the rights of nature were violated by the mining operations, which were polluting the nearby rivers. This case was different from the previous case in that the government was addressing the violation of the rights of nature. The court's decision was also swiftly enforced, as a military operation to destroy the machinery used for illegal mining was ordered and implemented (Daly, 2012).

6.2   USA (Pennsylvania)

On 8 August 2014, the Little Mahoning River (Figure 6.2) and its watershed successfully 'intervened' in a lawsuit (*PGE v. GT*, 2014) to prevent the lifting of a ban on injecting fracking wastewater into wells (Babcock, 2016). This was the first case in the history of the United States that a watershed had participated as an intervenor with a "kind of personhood" (La Follette and Maser, 2017: 80) in a legal system in its own name to protect its right to

Figure 6.2 Little Mahoning River
(By Jakec – Own work, CC BY-SA 4.0)[10]

"exist, flourish and naturally evolve" (Grant Township Community Bill of Rights Ordinance, 2014: Section 2 Clause d). Although a permit was eventually granted and a later court (*PGE v. GT*, 2015) overturned the decision made on 8 August 2014 and sidestepped the issue of standing for nature, the case was groundbreaking. It was the first 'rights of nature' action in the USA where the intervenor was a watershed.

6.3   India

Days after the high court in India's Uttarakhand state had issued a landmark judgement (*Salim v. State of Uttarakhand and Others*, 2017) declaring the Ganges as a 'living entity', Brij Khandelwal called the Agra police to report an attempted murder. Khandelwal, an environmental activist, followed the logic that "scientifically speaking, the Yamuna is ecologically dead" (Safi, 2017: online). His police report (a First Information Report or 'FIR') named a series of government officials he wanted to be charged with attempted poisoning and stated: "If the river is dead, someone has to be responsible for killing it" (Safi, 2017: online).

Although this judgement (*Salim v. State of Uttarakhand and Others*, 2017) is currently 'stayed' and the response of the police is unknown, both actions demonstrate the potential of juristic personhood to safeguard the biophysical integrity of spiritual-natural entities.

In order for the juristic personhood of spiritual-natural entities to become more acceptable to the courts, it seems clear that more litigation is required.

6.4   Gaining judicial traction for 'rights of nature' and juristic personhood

In the USA the Community Environmental Legal Defence Fund (CELDF) has been spearheading Community Rights Networks, which allow communities under environmental threat to pass 'rights of nature' ordinances. The group has been involved in dozens of grassroots campaigns, including the drafting of ecosystem rights in the (2008) Ecuador constitution (Charman, 2008). In addition to assisting people in Ecuador and Bolivia, CELDF has been working in Nepal and India, and with communities in the USA, Canada, Mexico, Ireland, Ghana, Cameroon, Australia, Colombia and the UK. In 2016, the Green Party of England and Wales worked with CELDF to include rights of nature in its official party platform (*The Ecologist*, 29/2/2016).

Despite the sanctions CELDF is facing in some parts of Pennsylvania, the adoption of Bills of Rights in other states could guarantee townships the authority to enact local laws to protect the environment, free from state pre-emption and corporate interference. Organisers in New Hampshire, Colorado, Oregon and Ohio are working to advance such rights. If they succeed, it will allow municipalities to litigate against frack wells, oil and gas extraction, and frack wastewater injection wells. The more of these cases that are heard in court and the more cases that judges review, the higher the likelihood that standing for nature will become normative, especially as more guidelines become available (Schromen-Wawrin, 2018).

Natural Justice (Lawyers for Communities and the Environment) is a young and fast-paced non-profit organisation specialising in environmental and human rights law in Africa in pursuit of social and environmental justice. Natural Justice comprises a team of pioneering lawyers and legal experts who offer direct support to communities that are impacted by the ever-increasing demand for land and resources, and conduct comprehensive research on environmental and human rights laws and engage in key national and international processes.

One suggestion (Sochaczewski, 2017, pers. comm., 3 Sept) is that law students assist Indigenous NGOs with test cases on a *pro bono* basis but supported by foundations or law faculties. Both Native Hawaiians and the Ktunaxa Nation could potentially benefit from test cases brought on their behalf in order to defend Mount Mauna Kea and Jumbo Valley.

Having reviewed the legal status of ecosystems, in general, it is important to understand the role of ritual protection of SNS as a behavioural practice by lay people, which is illustrated in the next chapter from research in the Tibetan region of Kham.

Notes

1 *Byram River v. Village of Port Chester,* 394 F. Supp. 618 (S.D.N.Y. 1975).
2 *Sun Enterprises v. Train,* 394 F. Supp. 211 (S.D.N.Y. 1975), *aff 'd,* 532 F.2d 280 (2d. Cir. 1976).
3 *Sun Enterprises v. Train,* 394 F. Supp. 211 (S.D.N.Y. 1975), *aff 'd,* 532 F.2d 280 (2d. Cir. 1976).
4 *Life of the Land, Inc. v. Bd. of Water Supply* (2d Cir. Hawaii) (filed Nov. 24, 1975).
5 *Death Valley Nat'l Monument v. Dept. of the Interior* (N.D. Cal.) (filed Feb. 26, 1976).
6 *Hookway et al. v. United States Department of Transportation* – the action arose from a complaint to enjoin a road realignment that would affect Billerica town common (Mass.) in violation of the National Environmental Policy Act; the action was not filed after a press conference and a threat of suit persuaded the Department of Transportation to modify its plans (Stone, 2010).
7 *Ezer v. Fuchsloch,* 160 Cal. Rptr. 486 (Ct. App. 1979).
8 *Palila v. Hawaii Dept. of Land & Natural Res.,* 471 F. Supp. 985 (D. Haw. 1979).
9 Mauna Kea Forest Restoration Project, undated, Palila https://dlnr.hawaii.gov/restoremaunakea/palila/
10 Jacek (2014), *Mahoning Creek below Kase Run* https://commons.wikimedia.org/w/index.php?curid=34170032

7 Case study

Ritual protection of SNS in the Tibetan region of Kham (southwest China)

Attempting to understand the status and nature of sacred natural sites is a complex process because it is typically predicated on spiritual/human agency, spiritual/human governance and ontic/epistemic modalities of engagement. Most of the widely read and cited peer-reviewed journal articles (referred to as 'the RC Literature') on sacred natural sites in the Eastern Kham region (see Table 7.2) have tended to focus on the 'metrics of biodiversity', and they have understated the role of lay people in the ritual protection of enspirited SNS under the aegis of "mountain cults" (Blondeau and Steinkellner, 1998: viii).

In order to fully represent or portray the eco-spiritual nature of sacred natural sites, it is seemingly necessary to combine the metrics of biodiversity with a detailed cultural and historical analysis among all stakeholders but especially among village-based lay people. Furthermore, in the multi-ethnic context of southwest China, the findings need to be disaggregated by ethnic group and reference made to local environmental perception, the status of SNS and the engagement (or familiarity) of local people with the endogenous processes that support ritual protection.

7.1 Kham

Kham is one of the most unique biological regions on earth. It is situated at the eastern end of the Himalaya between Qinghai-Tibetan plateau and China. The region constitutes about 4% of China's land area, includes seven mountain ranges and comprises Western Kham (Figure 7.1) and Eastern Kham (separated by the Yangtze River).

Kham's spectacular north-south mountain ridges sandwiched between deep river gorges contain the most diverse vascular plant flora of any region of comparable size in the temperate zone and almost half of China's flowering plant species. Identified as one of twenty-five biodiversity hotspots on earth (Myers et al., 2000), this vast region, covering 414,400 sq km, contains over 12,000 species of vascular plants, including 3,500 species

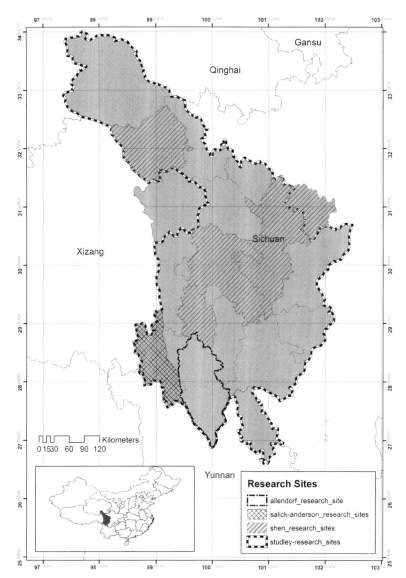

Figure 7.1 Eastern Kham Region showing research sites and an insert of China

which are found nowhere else. Although some botanical exploration has been conducted, the region has never been fully inventoried because of the sensitive political environment and the rugged terrain, which makes much of the area difficult to traverse.

Table 7.1 Most widely read and cited peer-reviewed journal articles

Author	Google scholar	Mendeley read	Mendeley cited	Researchgate read	Researchgate cited	TOTAL
Salick et al. (2007)	122	130	72	72	111	507
Anderson et al. (2005)	101	84	57	25	86	353
Allendorf et al. (2014)	15	10	0	170	11	206
Shen et al. (2015)	0	25	1	104	2	132
Shen et al. (2012)	24	7	16	44	23	114

Elevations range from 1000m to over 7556m with a mean elevation of 3500m. Four of Asia's largest rivers[1] flow through the region, which originates on the 5000m-high Qinghai-Tibetan plateau, and are of great economic importance to the people who live along them. External impact on the region is increasing and poses a threat to Tibetan culture and religion. Two examples of this impact include (1) tree mining between 1950 and 1998, which resulted in flooding, climate change, erosion and snow disasters; and (2) resettlement by outsiders. Such activities threaten not only the diversity of flora and fauna but also the survival of Indigenous cultures that define much of Southeast Asia.

The region bears the strong imprint of Tibetan Buddhism and Animistic folk religion, evident in the large temple complexes, *chortens* (which are spelt *mchod rten*), prayer flags, festivals, shaman and *numina* associated with sacred landscape features. Sacred mountains punctuate the landscape, and they are unique in that many of their forests have not been logged to the same extent as adjacent lands (Coggins and Hutchinson, 2006). Although more ethnobotanical research has been done in this region than in the rest of China, little research has been conducted into customary 'nature conservation' practices, linguistic ecologies, environmental perceptions, environmental values or the impact of proposed landscape use changes on the local people.

7.2   Peoples of Eastern Kham

Kham is one of the most bioculturally diverse regions on earth, and it is bisected by an ethnic corridor (Fei Xiaotong, 1980, cited in Sun, 1990) on the eastern edge of the Tibetan Plateau (see Figure 7.2). Of nearly 5 million Tibetans (Chin. *zangzu*) living in China, there are approximately 2 million

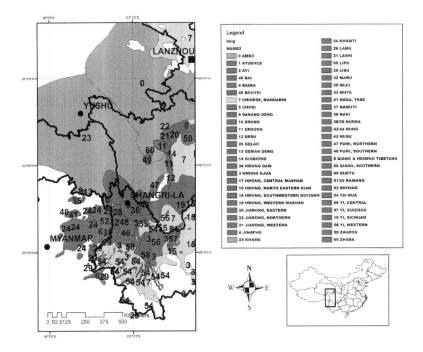

Figure 7.2 China's western ethnic corridor

(Modified by Studley in 2016 from www.muturzikin.com/cartesasie/9.htm and http://sichuan zoulang.com/en/)

who speak Kham. They inhabit a vast area but are primarily concentrated "for political and historical reasons in western Sichuan Province, a large portion of eastern Tibet, parts of southern Qinghai Province, and parts of Northern Yunnan. The eastern Kham language is by far the largest of the Kham varieties with possibly 1,250,000 speakers" (Studley, 2007: 29). It is reported to have at least eight dialects and 80% lexical similarity with central Tibetan (Studley, 2005).

There are also about 333,000 Qiangic-speaking peoples (Ergong, Ersu, Guiqiong, Jiarong, Minyak or Muya, Namuyi, Northern Pumi, Queyu, Shixing, Zhaba and Heishui Tibetans) in Eastern Kham. The Qiangic-speaking peoples are classified by the state as Tibetan (or *zangzu*) because of their culture, customs and beliefs.[2] In common with the Khambas, they are Animistic and shamanistic as well as Tibetan Buddhist and burn incense and honour mountain gods at yearly festivals. They may speak Khamba as a second or third language and are often matrilineal.

Table 7.2 Tibetan history

Date		
10,200–3000 BC	Neolithic/Iron Age Era	The Genesis of the mundane divinity cults (*yul-lha* and *gzhi bdag*) with origins in the Animistic High Asian steppe culture and the domestication of yak (Bellezza, 2005).
ca 5c BC	Bon culture introduced	Torpa Shenrab introduces Bon into Zhang Zhung (West Tibet) and mythically 'tames' the local mountain divinities (Bellezza, 2005; Ermakov, 2008; Samuel, 1993).
221–206 BC	Qin Dynasty (China)	The Qin persecute the Qiangic-speaking peoples who migrate to the Eastern Edge of the Tibetan Plateau (Ah Xiang, 1998).
127–104 BC	King Nyatri Tsenpo (1)	The Zhang Zhung alphabet is created using three scripts – wild, big and small (Dakpa, 2006) – and Bon teachings are written in the Zhang Zhung script (Ermakov, 2008).
11–32 AD	King Drigum Tsenpo (8)	First persecution of Bonpo – Bon banished to the periphery of Tibet (Dakpa, 2006).
525–550 AD	King Thothori Nyantsen (28)	First Dissemination of Buddhism (Powers, 2007); a basket of Buddhist scriptures arrived in Tibet from India (Ourvan, 2016).
618–649 AD	King Songtsan Gampo (33)	The King conquers the Zhang Zhung kingdom, which is integrated into Tibet in 645 AD (Schaeffer et al., 2013). The King sends Sambhota to Kashmir in 632 AD to bring back a written language (Handa, 2001), which is an adaption of Khotanese based on the Brahmi and Gupta scripts (Berzin, 2013). Buddhist scriptures translated into Tibetan (Keown and Prebish, 2013).
740–797 AD	King Trisong Detsen (38)	The King invites Shantarakshita to establish Buddhism (Dongyal, 2008) and Guru Rinpoche visits Tibet and brings "all the local gods under his command" (Zangpo, 2002).
		Second persecution of Bonpo – Bon banished to the periphery of Tibet (Dakpa, 2006).
836 AD	King Ralpachen assassinated by Langdarma	This lead to the persecution of Buddhism, the breakup of the Tibetan Empire and eventually to the sub-division of Tibet into two kingdoms (929 AD) by Langdarma's sons (Stein, 1972).

Date		
1042 AD	King Tsenpo Khorey/King Song Ngey of the Ngari region of western Tibet	Ex-King Tsenpo Khoray (who abdicates to become a monk – named Yeshe) sends his nephew Jangchub to invite Dipamkara Shrijnana Atisha to come to Western Tibet (Ngari). and he writes a book called *Lamp to the Path of Enlightenment* (Berzin, 2013). Although Tibet is still politically fragmented, Atisha's arrival in Tibet in 1042 marks the beginning of what is called the Second Dissemination of Buddhism in Tibet. Through Atisha's teachings and writings, Buddhism once again becomes the main religion of the people of Tibet (Keown and Prebish, 2013).
1360 AD	New or Modern Bon	The second Diffusion of Bon begins (Bowker, 2000; Hinnells, 1997; Samuel, 1993).
1391 AD	Dalai Lama dynasty begins	The First Dalai Lama is born (Mullin, 2005).
1966–1976	Cultural Revolution	The mundane divinity cults almost become extinct, trance mediums (*lha-pa*) are persecuted and ritual cairns (*la btsas*) are destroyed (Karmay, 1998; Karmay, 2004).
1978	'Religious Revival'	Hu Yaobang visits Tibet and is shocked by conditions and at the 3rd plenum of the 11th Party Congress measures introduced for the 'revival' of religious expression (Luo, 1991).
The 1980s	Recovery of folk practices	Gradual spontaneous recovery of folk practices, including the *gzhi bdag* cult (Schwartz, 1994) – this has been accompanied by biodiversity recovery in ISNS.
1998	Felling Ban	A felling ban is introduced in southwest China as a result of annual serious flooding of the main rivers in the region (Studley, 1999).

Important events in the history of the lay people of Tibet

The Kham-ba[3] have "a fearsome reputation as the most hostile and violent of Tibetans. They have been described as tall and well-built men, fearless and open of countenance. They resemble Apache Indians, with plaited hair hanging from each side of well-modelled heads" (Hattaway, 2000: 127).

The region's inhospitable topography, altitude, weather and aggressive population have always 'united' to deny entry to foreigners. Even today, few accurate maps define its contours, record its villages and map the secret routes of its nomads. To the Europeans, Chinese and Lhasa Tibetans, Kham has always been a vast no-man's land. To the south, it is bounded by the Himalaya and the Brahmaputra, to the north the Amne Machin range and the Tibetan region of Amdo, and to the east the Sichuan Basin.

It is important not to conflate ethnic groups who live in Kham as most of them have unique ethnolinguistic profiles and environmental perception (Studley, 2005).

7.3   History

Space only allows for a summary of the history of Kham (see Studley, 2003 and Table 7.3). It is hardly surprising that here in this wild, forgotten land should be found one of the most rugged races on earth and an independent fighting spirit that was birthed during the reign of Tibetan King Songtsen Gampo (AD 617–650). Songtsen Gampo was a Tibetan chieftain who set out to unify the wild tribes of central Asia in AD 630. Twenty years after taking up arms, he had raised one of the fiercest armies of all time and extended his empire over Kham and Amdo, which had been the domain of the White Wolf Qiang, as well as most of central Asia and well into China (Marshall and Cooke, 1997).

From the frightened Chinese emperor, he "demanded a daughter in marriage. The emperor was obliged to comply and also to pay an annual tribute to the Tibetan King" (Studley, 2007: 30). So powerful was Tibet at this time that when in AD 763 a subsequent Chinese emperor refused to pay the 50,000 rolls of silk owed in tribute to the Tibetan court, Trisong Detson, Songtsen Gampo's great-grandson, invaded China and captured Xi'an, the capital of the Celestial Empire. The Tibetan king then deposed the Chinese emperor and replaced him temporarily with his own brother-in-law. In AD 821, during a lull in hostilities, Tibet and China made a pact of non-aggression (Stein, 1972). Later when King Ralpachen was assassinated (836 AD), the Tibetan empire began to disintegrate, and Kham became more independent.

In the 1,200 years that followed, however, the history of Kham was marked by endless feuds between warrior chiefs in deadly competition for supremacy over Kham's remote hinterlands (Lane, 1994). By the end of the 12th century, the Kingdom of Ling, home of the epic hero King Gesar, had expanded to include most of Kham, if we are to believe his 'superhuman' exploits (Samuel, 2002). In the 1600s the Naxi Kings[4] felt strong enough to make incursions into Tibetan territory, resulting in recurrent fighting on the southern Kham cultural-ecological frontier. This made the Tibetans build watch and defence towers across southern Kham separating the Tibetans from the Tibeto-Burmans

Table 7.3 Tibetan culture

Tutelery Deities	Celestial Deities	Mundane Deities	Malevolent Spirits
1. TIBETAN GODS AND SPIRITS (Samuel, 1993)			
2. THREE RELIGIOUS TRADITIONS (Powers, 2007)			
lha-chos – Tibetan Buddhism		mi-chos – 'man's religion' – mundane deities	bon-chos – Bon (Yangdrung and 'Modern')
3. THREE CLASSES OF MUNDANE DEITY (Karmay, 1998)			
Yul-lha – gods who preside over settlements and human activity typically in a watershed		gzhi-bdag – numina spirits who inhabit the middle slopes of most mountains	klu – numina spirits who live in lakes, rivers and ponds
4. TWO CULTURAL POLES IN EACH VILLAGE/COMMUNITY (Karmay, 1998)			
Tibetan Buddhist or Bon cult		Animistic mundane deity cult	
5. TWO SACRED LANDSCAPE CATEGORIES (Huber, 1999)			
'Epistemic' virtual landscapes, presided over by celestial gods and imagined or contrived by Tibetan Buddhism/Bonpo (Huber, 1999)		'Ontic' Animistic landscapes inhabited by a gzhi bdag that are real and experienced by lay people on the basis of cult participation, autochthony and belonging (Lightfoot, 1986; Eliade, 1959) – all concepts which are alien to Tibetan Buddhism.	
6. MOUNTAIN STRATIFICATION (Punzi, 2014)			
Summit – presided over by celestial gods		Middle Slopes – inhabited by gzhi bdag	Valleys – human domain – presided over by a yul lha

(Continued)

Table 7.3 (Continued)

7. FOUR TYPES OF LOCAL GOVERNANCE OF SNS

Monastic – who regulate behaviour in monastic lands and mountains they have co-opted and tamed (and have become pilgrimage sites)	*Sui generis* – ad hoc patrols (known as *ri bsher*) by lay people protect the SNS from trespassers and hunters from other communities/ kinship groups	Spiritual – *gzhi bdag* are owners and de jure/de facto custodians of the SNS and their clients comply with their behavioural expectations within the SNS	Sealed enclosures (*ri rgya*) are the result of a formal ritual presided over by lamas and headmen and are often superimposed on *gzhi bdag* domains.

8. MOTIVATION MODES FOR VISITING SNS

TB/Bon visit SNS so they can engage in spiritual exercises that ground their faith and help them concentrate on self-purification on an inner journey leading to inner peace	Lay people – visit SNS to honour and appease their *gzhi bdag* and to experience the ontic realities of participating and belonging to a local autochthonomous cult	Outsider's Perception – 'Mountain or SNS Worship'

9. DESIGNATED SNS (Buckley, 2007)

SNS designated by monasteries under the aegis of TB/Bon 'visionary' landscaping.	SNS designated by villagers as directed by the *gzhi bdag* (Limusishiden, 2014)

Important categories for Tibetan lay people

(van Spengen, 2002). The kingdom of Ling must have declined because it apparently played no significant role in 1640 during Gushri Khan's campaigns in Kham when his principal opponent was the pro-Bon King of Beri.

By the 17th century, the kingdom of Derge had enlarged itself at Ling's and Beri's expense, and subsequently, much of eastern Kham became part of the extensive Derge estate. It would appear, however, that Ling and Beri continued as semi-independent states. In spite of Derge's overlordship, eastern Kham's nomads were notorious for their independent nature, and they could hardly be considered submissive to anyone except their immediate tribal chiefs. When, as occasionally happened, a foreigner was foolish enough to challenge the Kham-bas, they would unite, and their quarrels momentarily were forgotten. When this occurred there were few who could oppose the "race of kings": not the Chinese, or even *Chinggis Khan*, who eventually came to terms with them on the basis of patron-priest relationship (Peissel, 1972: 11).

7.4   Kham-ba identity

Kham-ba identity (and place attachment) is germane in the context of this book because it is rooted in the local *gzhi bdag* cults and the ritual protection of SNS (Studley, 2012). Kham is situated between two power centres, China and Tibet. From the late 19th to the mid-20th century, imperial, colonial and local forces clashed and intersected in a process of place-making and nation-building (Epstein, 2002). Too often latter-day Chinese, Tibetan and Western accounts have ignored this and peripheralised local concerns. Recent research, however, has begun to address aspects of the axes of power, space and identity in Kham, the often-discordant visions of parties who wished to transform it, and the vision of the Khamba. Traditional history characterised Kham as a frontier zone to be incorporated and civilised by the centres of power. In traditional studies of frontier places, the people who inhabit them have been portrayed as passive objects, and their responses to forces beyond their immediate control simply ignored. When viewed from the centres of power (Beijing, Chengdu and Lhasa), frontier zones like Kham were easily relegated to the margins of history. This position has been interrogated increasingly in the recent scholarship of the Han frontier and has led to a re-centring of the local. The Kham-bas have been employing "political strategies which appropriated both local and inflowing resources, thus turning them into power sources and establishing their sense of centrality" (Epstein, 2002: 2).

Although most ethnographic and historical studies focus on central Tibet, with the exception of King Gesar of Ling, it would appear that Kham did not make much impression on the Tibetan or Chinese consciousness until the mid-nineteenth century with the Khamba warlord *nyag rong mgon po mam rgyal (mgon mam)* and Chinese and Tibetan activities in the border region. However, there is strong indication that even before this period there was an emergent national consciousness among the Khambas, of which *mgon mam* was only a part. During the Republican period (AD 1911–1949) there were three movements for Khamba autonomy (Peng Wenbin, 2002) – the Baan incident in 1932, the Nuola incident in 1935 and the Ganzi (*kandze*) incident in 1939 – but they were largely written out of standard Chinese and Tibetan histories. In reality, the Kham-bas' actions were mapped in response to politics in Central Tibet and China. They were attempting to establish regional autonomy while coping with Chinese and Tibetan nation-building projects (Feng Youzhi, 1992). There has been little research exploring *mgon mam*'s attempt to restructure society and build a Khamba state (Tsering, 1985), the religious and philosophical union resulting from the *ris med* movement or the revival of the King Gesar cult as the foundational saga for unification (Samuel, 2002). Taken together, these movements appear to signal a nascent sense of unique Khamba identity (Epstein, 2002; Samuel, 1993), which continues to this day. This identity provides the basis for rituals of defiance and protests articulated in the *gzhi bdag* cult (Schwartz, 1994).

7.5   Cultural context

For the exigencies of daily life, many Tibetan lay people are Animistic, and they typically participate in mountain or *gzhi bdag* cults, which are classified under the aegis of *mi chos* ('the religion of men'). They honour and appease the *gzhi bdag*, and they ritually protect their domain (and flora/ fauna), typically on the middle slopes of village-designated mountains on the basis of contractual reciprocity. In contrast to Tibetan Buddhism and Bon followers, as *gzhi bdag* cult members they benefit from the "lived or living experience" (Ingold, 2000: 1) and "ontic realities" (Daniel, 1996: 27) of being, participating and belonging to an autochthonous (native) and unique expression of Tibetaness (see Table 7.4).

Table 7.4 Engagement and familiarity with the *gzhi bdag* cults and ritual protection of SNS

Are you Familiar with: n=12	*Answers to questions %*	*Mostly unknown (U) or volunteered (V) %*
gzhi bdag	100	
The number of *gzhi bdag* in this village	100	
The size of each *gzhi bdag* domain	90	
The liminal boundaries of the domain	100	
The concept of ritual sealing (U)		8.3

Are you Familiar with: n=12	Answers to questions %	Mostly unknown (U) or volunteered (V) %
The *gzhi bdag* rituals	83.33	
What guides behaviour in the domain (V)		42
What behaviour is allowed in the domain	100	
What behaviour is not allowed in the domain	75	
If retribution takes place for transgressors	50	
The types of restitution required to appease a *gzhi bdag*	75	
The modes of ritual enquiry (V)		25
The biodiversity status of the domain	83.33	
with unique flora/fauna present within the domain	66.66	
	84%	

7.6   Environmental perception

7.6.1   Traditional interactions with nature

The lay Tibetan beliefs that support the ritual protection of enspirited SNS, often described as "mountain cults" (Blondeau and Steinkellner, 1998: viii), have their origins in Neolithic steppe culture. Throughout history they have had to be discursively recalibrated as attempts have been made by the Bon religion (see Samuel, 1993), Tibetan Buddhism, Communism and modernity to assimilate them. In spite of localised assimilation and taming attempted under the aegis of "Buddhicisation" and "Bonicisation" (McKay, 2013: 7), mountain cults remain extant in almost every village in Eastern Kham to this day (Studley, 2014).

Regardless of assimilation, there appears to be a strong tradition of local-ised 'environmental protection' among the people that live in Eastern Kham, and unique "linguistic ecologies" (Muhlhausler, 2002: 22) bear testimony to these traditions. Of those studied, in Ninglang County (Studley, 2007), the Tibetan, Pumi, Naxi and Mosuo appear to have the strongest traditions of protection[5], followed by the Nosu (Yi) and Han. There appears to be evidence of what conservationists would call explicit nature conservation in some locales.

As "keepers of culture" (Zevik, 2002: 200), Eastern Kham's 'shaman' and priests are often "knowledgeable about trees, plants and animals and play an important role in environmental storytelling and mediation. While the priests are mostly interested in other-worldly religion, the shaman are liminal beings ensuring harmony within the cosmos" (Studley, 2007: 33).

The 'shaman' in Eastern Kham, including the Tibetan *Lha-pa*, the Naxi *Dongba*, the Mosuo *Daba* and the Pumi *Dingba*, all perform similar functions to the Qiang *Shibi*, the Hunza/Gilgat *Bitan*, the Jumla *Dharmi* and the Bhutan *Powa/nenjorm*. The priests include the Nosu (Yi) *Bimo*, Tibetan Buddhist *Lamas* (attached to monasteries) and local *Lamas*[6].

Although the Tibetan *Lha-pa*, Mosuo *Daba*, Naxi *Dongba* and Pumi *Dingba* continue to have a role in environmental education (Yang Fuquan, 2003), their role has diminished because their skills are not being transferred inter-generationally. Although attempts have been made to revitalise their role through mentoring and training, it has proved challenging to retain young apprentices who find tourism more attractive (Yang Fuquan, 2003).

Sacred natural sites are a common phenomenon throughout West China from Dai Holy Hills in Southern Yunnan (Pei Shengji, 1993) to Tibetan "sacred mountains" (Xu et al., 2005: online). Most ethnic groups (Studley, 2007) were able to identify sacred mountains, trees, animals and springs and could describe the protection measures they were expected to adopt to ensure blessing and protection from the *numina* associated with territory or landscape features. Lion Mountain in Ninglang County is particularly auspicious for the Mosuo, and all ethnic groups believe *Gemu* (the goddess of Lion Mountain) has been violated by the introduction of a cable car (Studley, 2003). They assume there is a causal link between her violation and the unseasonal hail and pine tree defoliation that occurred in 2004 (Rowcroft et al., 2006).

The Kham-ba Tibetans have three categories of sacred geography. Two are Buddhist and include *kora* (pilgrimage) mountains and 'beyul' (spelt *sbas yul)* valleys (which are sacred 'hidden' landscapes, epitomised by *Shangri-la*). The other is Animistic, namely, enspirited landscapes which are inhabited by a *gzhi bdag* with human personality (Blondeau and Steinkellner, 1998) and characterised by the ritual protection.

7.6.2   Nature ethics

In common with many Indigenous people, there is a tradition of spirit-placation/community restitution based on maintaining relational harmony in Eastern Kham. The Tibetan, Mosuo and Pumi all described the measures required to placate local *numina* and make restitution with the local community when trees or animals were killed in sacred areas intentionally or by mistake (Studley, 2007).

Although the Buddhist canon teaches that life is sacred and the Buddhist purgatory includes a special cold hell for souls who have killed animals, the Tibetans have always been avid hunters. They have accepted, however, that there are some 'taboos' in some locations and species, and they don't want to anger the local gods. Hunting appears to have been accepted by the establishment when game was plentiful, if there was a demand for furs in the monasteries or from the elite, or for trading purposes in Eastern Kham (Combe, 1926). Ancient dramas, such as *Dunyudunju*, are still performed in which the hero learns the art of hunting. Tibetan laymen still seek the blessing and protection of their *gzhi bdag* when they go hunting (Bleisch and Wong, 1990).

For most Tibetans, the spiritual significance of 'conservation' or protection appears more important than the ecological significance. This finding is supported by research conducted in Ganzi Prefecture (Studley, 2005). It is not the biophysical elements of nature that are important but the topocosmic inter-relationship renders the resources (forest and wildlife) apparent and concrete (Lye, 2005; Nightingale, 2006).

Khamba respondents are evidently similar to some other Indigenous people in that they are not deliberate conservationists or ecologists, but they manifest an ethical attitude because nature has intrinsic value, having been created by or presided over by a deity or *numina*.

In common with the Sherpa Tibetans (Stevens, 1993; Stevens, 1997), the Khamba appear to recognise several different categories of forest steward-ship, from sacred and untouched to unmanaged and overexploited.

Tibetans who inadvertently remove material from a *gzhi bdag* habitat have an opportunity to make amends, usually by making offerings to the *gzhi bdag*. This reflects the emphasis on maintaining balance within the cosmoscape and not upsetting such systems through extreme or unusual actions. Villagers make frequent offerings to local deities to ensure bless-ing; additional offerings may be used to rectify a disturbance. An even more explicit form of restitution is replanting trees that have been cut down or taken away. This attempts to restore the disturbed area to its former integrity. The belief is that once the trees have grown back, the health and well-being of the culprit and the community will be restored. The replanting of trees is generally at the instruction of a *Lha-pa*.

Although Tibetans appear to engage in *rtsi shing tshe thar* or tree 'free-ing' ceremonies (Figure 7.3), which results in the tree's protection (Awang, 2014, pers. comm., 3 Dec; Lhamo Tsheskyid, 2012), they do not appear to have any specific tree/forest consecration (*byin brlabs*) ceremonies. Lay people, however, do recognise and ritually protect trees within the territory of their *gzhi bdag*, and forests associated with monasteries are typically 'robed' in cloth or thread in similar ways to some Thai or *Chipko* forests (Guha, 2000).

Figure 7.3 A tree that has been freed

(Permission from Awang)

7.7   The status of SNS and the *gzhi bdag* cult in Eastern Kham

There is evidence that many of the sacred natural sites of Southwest China are hotspots or refugia of biodiversity and that they and the endogenous processes that support them have partially recovered since China's religious revival in 1978 (see Table 7.3) based on the following findings:

There are greater differences between sacred and non-sacred sites in the Kawakarpo Mountains in terms of larger trees (DBH),[7] basal area[8] (m²/ha) and useful and endemic species (Anderson et al., 2005; Salick et al., 2007).

Approximately 25% of the Tibetan Plateau, 30% of Ganzi Tibetan Autonomous Prefecture and 60% of the Yubeng Valley, northwest Yunnan is comprised of sacred landscape (Buckley, 2007; Shen et al., 2012; Studley and Awang, 2016).

Deforestation in Danba County has decreased in SNS from 19.7ha per year (1974–1989) to 4.4ha per year (1999–2013) since China's religious revival in 1978 (Shen et al., 2015).

The Animistic lay beliefs that support the ritual protection of SNS are still extant in the region (Allendorf et al., 2014; Awang, 2014; Bum, 2016;

Studley, 2005, 2007, 2012, 2014; Studley and Awang, 2016; Woodhouse et al., 2015; Zhang, 2003, 2007).

There is at least one ritually protected *gzhi bdag* habitat in most Tibetan villages (Bum, 2016), and in Northwest Yunnan, there are 3.1 *gzhi bdag* habitats per village comprising 700ha (Studley and Awang, 2016).

Among lay people in Northwest Yunnan, there is on average 84% familiarity (see Table 7.5) with the *gzhi bdag* cult and the ritual protection of SNS (Studley and Awang, 2016).

7.8 Lay participation in the ritual protection of SNS in Eastern Kham (with special reference to Danba County)

The importance of lay participation in the "endogenous processes" (Apgar et al., 2011: 555) that underpin the nurturance of sacred natural sites has largely been understated in the most widely read and cited literature ('the RC Literature'), which is highlighted in the following critique.

7.8.1 *Ethnic differentiation*

Although it is fairly accurate[9] to say that "73.9% of the population of Danba County is 'Zangzu'" (Shen et al., 2015: 1520), the figures are largely predicated on a conflated minority nationality classification, and not on the basis of linguistics or DNA profiling. In reality in Danba County, "39% of the Zangzu are Tibetic-speakers (Rongbrag Kham and Amdo nomads) and 61% are Qiangic speakers – the Qiang, Jiarong, and Ergong" (Jinba, 2013: 14). The Qiangic-speaking *Zangzu* and the *Qiangzu*, in contrast to the Tibetans, belong to a matriarchal culture, share a bloodline with the ancient Xia people, have a DNA profile that is geographically discordant from the Tibetans and do not have the same environment values (Studley, 2005).

7.8.2 *China's religious revival and the recovery of* gzhi bdag *cults*

Although limited reference is made in the RC literature to China's "religious revival" (Shen et al., 2015: 1524), no detail is provided and no comment is made on its impact on folk beliefs and the subsequent spontaneous recovery of biodiversity in enspirited SNS.

In 1978 at the 3rd plenum of the 11th Party Congress, possibly as a result of Hu Yaobang's visit to Tibet in 1978 (Goldstein, 1997) and the failures of assimilation, measures were introduced to encourage religious revival (mostly mainstream religions), which was followed by new nationality

Figure 7.4 A trance medium or *lha pa*
(Permission from J. V. Bellezza)

policies of ethnic pluralism [1982] and autonomy [1984]. When a conference in Shanghai [1984] announced that there was no contradiction
between religion and socialism, many ethnic traditions, clan systems and
customs were re-vitalised and celebrated (Harrell, 2001), and a profound
nativisation of culture begun to take place, which included the spontaneous recovery of folk beliefs (Schwartz, 1994). As a result, Yunnan's Yi
peoples moved immediately to change the status of their priest or *bimo*
from a 'feudal superstitious practitioner' to ethnic intellectual and the
Tibetans revitalised their *gzhi bdag* cults and Tibetan Buddhism (Goldstein and Kapstein, 1998). Shaman and Trance mediums (see Figure 7.4),
however, were not accepted until 1994 (Cai Hua, 2001). These measures
allowed Tibetan lay people once again to participate in the ritual protection of mountains (inhabited by a *gzhi bdag*) and resulted in the recovery
of biodiversity.

7.8.3   The motivation for visiting sacred natural sites

There is very little endogenous evidence that Tibetans 'worship mountains'
(Studley, 2005), the divinities that inhabit them (Yeh and Lama, 2015) or
that "Tibetans have worshipped . . . sacred sites for centuries" (Shen et
al., 2012: online). It is also questionable (in Danba County or elsewhere)
to suggest that "mountain worship is deeply rooted in Bon" (Shen et al.,

2015: 1519), given that the Animistic mountain cults have their origins in Neolithic steppe culture, which pre-dates Yungdrung Bon, Modern Bon and Tibetan Buddhism (see Table 7.3).

Lay Tibetans are motivated to visit enspirited SNS (typically on the middle slopes of mountains) to honour and appease their *gzhi bdag* in much the same way that they would a King or Emperor, and they protect their mountain domains out of behavioural compliance (Studley, 2014). In addition, they engage in the ontic realities and living experience of participating and belonging to a local autochthonomous (native) mountain cult (Eliade, 1959).

In contrast, Tibetan Buddhists and 'modern' Bon-po visit tamed (Tib. *'dul ba*) and "mandalized" (Makley, 2007: 53) mountains so they can engage in spiritual exercises such as pilgrimage (Figure 7.5) that ground their faith and help them concentrate on self-purification on an inner journey leading to inner peace (McKay, 2013).

When Yungdrung Bon and Buddhism were first introduced (see Table 7.3) into Tibet, the first acts of Tenpo Shenrab[10] and Guru Rinpoche[11] was to try and tame the local mundane gods to give Bon and Buddhism more legitimacy (Bellezza, 2005). In reality as far as lay Tibetans are concerned, most mundane divinities and landscapes remain wild to this day (Studley, 2014), and even the so-called tamed mountains are usually inhabited by a *gzhi bdag*.

Figure 7.5 Pilgrims in Ganzi Prefecture
(Studley, photo taken in 2003)

7.8.4   The role of religious institutions in support of sacred natural sites

The RC literature suggests that "all Tibetan sacred sites have their associated monasteries" (Shen et al., 2012: online) and that monasteries play an important role in their protection and regulation (Salick et al., 2007; Shen et al., 2012, 2015), although this claim is not well supported by field research among lay people (Studley, 2014). Furthermore, the emphasis is placed on "strengthening formal religious institutions" (Shen et al., 2015: 1518), in order to enhance nature conservation; however, little detail is provided on the role of traditional beliefs, local mechanisms or *gzhi bdag* cults in environmental protection. This bias appears to favour orthodox religious institutions.

7.8.4.1   Tibetan Buddhist institutions

Although TB is not insensitive to the natural world, it is primarily preoccupied with emptiness (*sunyata*) and non-attachment (*ma chags pa*) and any ritual response to nature is at best secondary or symbolic (Eckel, 1998; Seeland, 1993). It is questionable how the role of Tibetan Buddhist institutions will help in the protection of SNS on mountains inhabited by a *gzhi bdag*. It might even be debatable if it is appropriate to attempt to harness Tibetan Buddhism for the purposes of conservation goals. Two eminent Japanese professors (Hakamaya Noriaki and Matsumoto Shiro) have stated that there is no basis for nature conservation or environmental protection in Orthodox Buddhism (Swanson, 1993). This is one reason (Darlington, 2000) that environmental monks in Thailand have had to draw on Animistic beliefs and "Dharmic socialism" (Buddhadasa, 1986: book title) to ensure the protection of the forest. Evidently, however, there are sensitivities in Buddhism that support nature conservation, and the recent trends among "Green Tibetans" (Huber, 1997: 103) are worth exploring.

7.8.4.2   Bon institutions

The Modern Bon religion is very localised and unheard of in much of southwest China (Studley, 2005). In Danba County (Figure 7.6), although most of the monasteries are Bon and 60% of the Jiarong are Bon-po (Jinba, 2016 pers. comm., 9 Jan), this only represents 12.6% of the population, or 10% of the Tibetan population of China (Bon, Wikipedia, 2005). There is little evidence that the Ergong, Rongbrag Kham, Qiang or Amdo nomads (i.e., 67.5% of the population) adhere to Bon. In contrast, all ethnolinguistic groups in Danba participate in the *gzhi bdag* cult (Jinba, 2016, pers. comm., 5 Jan).

It appears to be legitimate to question whether monasteries provide as much protection as some authors (e.g., Shen et al., 2015) seem to imply given the orientation of Bon and role of lay people in the protection of enspirited SNS on the middle slopes of most mountains in Danba County. In addition, it is questionable if most of the sacred mountains (especially those inhabited by a *gzhi bdag*) in Danba County are "close to monasteries" (Shen et al., 2015: 1519) given that 80% of mountains (4600m+)[12] are more than 10km from the main monasteries (see Figure 7.6).

Furthermore, it is questionable if Yungdrung or Modern Bon provides a conceptual basis for conservation or that there are any grounds to apply the term Bon to the mountain cults as they exist today (Samuel, 1993).

Yungdrung Bon has a celestial and mystical orientation predicated on the *sauvastika*, the moon, the feminine, Mithraism and gnostic advancement or *sgo-phug-pa* (Studley, 2016).

Modern Bon was introduced in 1360 AD (see Table 7.3) and has been heavily influenced by Mahayana Buddhism introduced from India (Bowker, 2000); it shares many common features (including the realisation of emptiness) with the Nyingma school of Tibetan Buddhism (Hinnells, 1997), and any connection with Yungdrung Bon is extremely tenuous (Bowker, 2000).

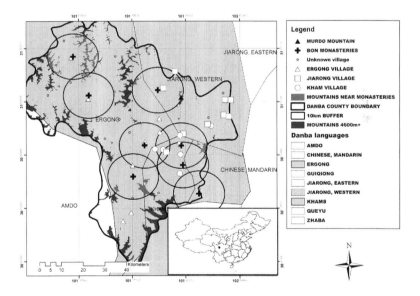

Figure 7.6 Danba County

(modified by Studley (2016) from www.muturzikin.com/cartesasie/9.htm and http://sichuan zoulang.com/en/)

Figure 7.7 A Khyung or Garuda

(Courtesy of Keith Dowman http://keithdowman.net/dzogchen/garuda.html)

As is typical, the Bon monks in one Danba monastery appear to honour a celestial solar deity named Khyung (Figure 7.7) on the summit of a mountain (Karmay and 長野泰彦, 2008). This gives the mountain imposed (or imagined) sacredness, but ritual protection is only secondary and not seemingly required by the divinity.

Although both Bon and Tibetan Buddhism have attempted to co-opt the mountain divinities, the *gzhi bdag* cult still remains today as a unique lay cultural expression in most villages, and it is questionable if strengthening the institutions of organised religion will help protect most of the SNS ritually protected by lay people (Studley, 2017a).

7.8.5   *The retention of SNS*

Although there is recognition in the RC literature that the "motivation for retaining sacred natural sites in a natural condition is not conservation" (Shen et al., 2015: 1524), there is little elaboration.

Until very recently there was no term for 'conservation' in Tibetan. The nearest cross-culturally equivalent concept used by lay people is *srung skyob* or *skyong*, which is translated as 'protection' or 'nurturance'. On the basis of cognitive mapping (Figure 7.8) conducted at 86 locations in Ganzi

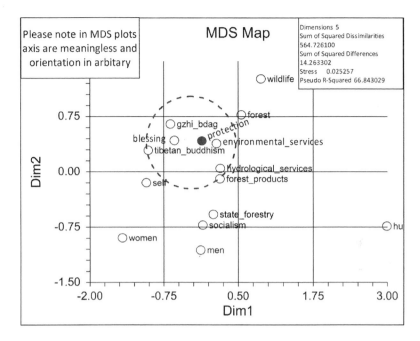

Figure 7.8 A cognitive map of environmental values
(Studley, 2005)

Prefecture (Studley, 2005), it would appear that a nexus of five concepts coalesces closely around *srung skyob* or *skyong*. These include *gzhi bdag*, blessing, environmental services, hydrological services and protection work by Tibetan Buddhists. This suggests that the concept of protection/ nurturance from a lay perspective embraces the *gzhi bdag* (and *gzhi bdag* domain), resulting in blessing and environmental/hydrological services and, in addition, includes 'nurturance' activities conducted by Tibetan Buddhists (e.g., tree planting by monasteries).

The protection nexus does not include *phyi rgyal srung skyob* (i.e., conservation by outsiders). This finding is supported by research at Lugu Lake (Rowcroft et al., 2006), where conservation was ranked number eighth out of thirteen environmental importance values (Table 7.5). Conservation is often regarded by Tibetans as a bio-centric intervention, which at best has a very limited interpretation of culture and at worst is guilty of cultural chauvinism. For most lay Tibetans, the Animistic spiritual importance of protection is more significant than the ecological importance of conservation (Callicott, 1989; Yeh and Lama, 2015).

Table 7.5 Local environmental importance ranking

Importance (n= 54)	Constant sum scaling[13] means
Life-Sustaining	14.1
Intrinsic	11.3
Subsistence	10.43
Aesthetic	9.43
Therapeutic	9.28
Future	9
Learning	7.86
Conservation	6.7
Commercial	5.28
Spiritual	4.43
Cultural	4.43
Historic	4.28
Recreational	3.43

Conservation or protection cannot be abstracted from the Indigenous reality of "belonging to nature" (Sponsel, 2012: xi), and the behaviour that lay people exhibit in/towards an SNS is predicated on the maintenance of *snod bcud do mnyam* (topocosmic equilibrium) among the human, natural and spiritual dimensions (Yeh and Lama, 2015).

7.8.6   What does sacred mean in the context of landscapes?

Although reference is made to 'sacred' in the RC literature (Anderson et al., 2005; Shen et al., 2012, 2015), it is not explicitly defined in relation to landscape with the exception of local appellations (Salick et al., 2007). Perhaps this may explain why there are not larger differences between non/sacred sites in the Kawakarpo Mountains. There is recognition that from a Tibetan perspective that "the entire metaphysical landscape is considered sacred" (Salick et al., 2007: 694) and that the designations of sacred and non-sacred are "clumsy and problematic" (Salick et al., 2007: 702). It is questionable, though, if a "gradient of sanctity" (Salick et al., 2007: 702) helps to define sacred. No reference (see Table 7.4) is made to the differences between assumed and imposed sacredness (Huber, 1999), ontic or epistemic sacred landscapes (Lightfoot, 1986; Eliade, 1959), or landscapes inhabited and enspirited by a *gzhi bdag*.

One of the problems with the term 'sacred' is that it does not necessarily equate to explicit nature conservation or greater biodiversity. The Khumbu Valley (Nepal) is regarded as a sacred *beyul* because the Guru Rinpoche hid it away "to be discovered by the Sherpas" (Brautigam, 2011: 13), but that does not mean that all the flora/fauna are protected. There are examples of ritually protected and biodiverse forests but also overexploited, unmanaged ones as well. The Sherpa lay people engage with their sacred landscape on the basis of "dynamic homeostasis" (Stevens, 1993: 268).

In the author's quest within the region (1999–2005) for exemplars of behaviour that equated to explicit nature conservation, he abandoned the term 'sacred' in favour of 'enspirited SNS' (Studley, 2014) because it denotes a landscape inhabited and owned by a *numina* (*gzhi bdag*) that are ritually protected on the basis of contractual reciprocity and ontic engagement and is an autochthonous (native) expression of Tibetan identity.

7.8.7 *Mountain stratification*

Shen et al. (2015: 1523) state that "the summits of mountains are the most sacred", but they fail to mention that in terms of biodiversity, the middle slopes appear to be more germane to explicit environmental protection.

Most of the mountains in the region are characterised by spiritual stratification, with the summit being presided over by a celestial divinity, the middle slopes being inhabited by a *gzhi bdag* and the valley (and settlements) being presided over by a settlement deity or *yul-lha*.

The summits have imputed or imposed sacredness (Huber, 1999), but environmental protection is only symbolic and not seemingly required by the presiding celestial divinity.

The middle slopes of mountains are typically the domains of the *gzhi bdag* and are characterised by ontic sacredness (Eliade, 1959), where the local lay people are expected to comply with the divinities' demands by not disturbing the domain and protecting the flora and fauna, on the basis of contractual reciprocity.

7.8.8 *Designation of SNS?*

Although reference is made to sacred natural sites in the RC literature (Anderson et al., 2005; Salick et al., 2007; Shen et al., 2012, 2015), there is no apparent attempt to categorise them on the basis of *bskog zhag* or designation.

Li Shengzhi (Buckley, 2007: 1) concluded after extensive research in Ganzi Tibetan Autonomous Prefecture that

> Traditionally every Tibetan village and monastery has designated its own sacred sites . . mountains . . where wildlife and land are protected.

This finding is supported on the basis of the author's research in every county in Ganzi Prefecture (Studley, 2005). In addition, the author discovered in each village in Shangri-la County (northwest Yunnan) that there are typically 3.1 designated sacred natural sites on the middle slopes of mountains that are all inhabited by a *gzhi bdag* and all ritually protected (Studley, 2014).

The designation and demarcation of village-based SNS, which are demarcated by a *la btsas*, occurs in concert between villagers and their *gzhi bdag* and traditionally with the help of a trance medium (Limusishiden, 2014). The *la btsas* is the *pho brang*, or palace of the *gzhi bdag*, and the structures form the centre of communal *la btsas* rituals that reinforce the exclusive relationship between a *gzhi bdag*, his (or her) local community and the community's territory (Tsering, 2016).

Most mountains in Southwest China are inhabited by a *gzhi bdag*, which is classified as a mundane divinity (or *'jig-rten-pa'i-srung-ma*) that is recognised by most Tibetan and Qiangic-speaking ethnic groups and is not associated with Tibetan Buddhism, Bon or monasteries (Huber, 1999).

The most important mountain in Danba County (which is made of solid quartz) is known as *dmu rdo gzhi bdag* because it is inhabited by a *gzhi bdag* who is the most important divinity in the region. Both the divinity and mountain were co-opted by Tibetan Buddhists and Bonpo, and the mountain is designated (i.e., given precious status) by all three traditions.

7.8.9   Governance of sacred natural sites

Although reference is made in the RC literature to the role of monasteries in maintaining local regulations addressing environmental protection (Shen et al., 2012, 2015), this claim is not well supported by field research among lay people in village-designated ritually protected SNS (Studley, 2014).

In much of southwest China, there appear to be four modes of local governance of sacred natural sites, namely spiritual governance, ad hoc *sui generis*, monastic and *ri rgya* (see Table 7.4 and Studley, 2014).

7.8.9.1   Spiritual governance

Spiritual governance is autochthonous (native) and predicated solely on the agency of *numina* (or *gzhi bdag*). The *numina* decide on the objectives of governance and their pursuance and orchestrate through intermediaries the decision-making process. Spiritual governance has more resonance with the spiritually guided governance of Plato (Fowler 1921) than the anthropocentric governance found in the international development literature (UNESCAP, 2009) or in the conservation literature (Borrini-Feyerabend and Hill, 2015).

The *gzhi bdag* that inhabit Indigenous sacred natural sites are not only place owners (*gzhi* = place), but as *bdag* [*po*], meaning 'Lords' or 'Governors', they hold absolute power and authority (Mills, 2003) of the mountain abodes over which they have dominion and jurisdiction. Their power extends to their genealogical titles, which suggest a strong sense of spiritual kinship with humankind. Furthermore, they are *de jure/de facto* custodians of all the biophysical resources within their domain (Studley, 2005). Their *modus operandi* of interaction with humankind is predicated on contractual reciprocity in which humankind does not hold a place of natural authority. The *gzhi bdag* agree to provide patronage, governance, blessing and protection if humankind honours and appeases them regularly and complies with their behavioural expectations in terms of protecting their property (including *flora/fauna*), especially when visiting their abode (Studley, 2014).

The primary objective of spiritual governance by all the participants is predicated on the maintenance of equilibrium among the human, biophysical and spirit worlds. Participants in this case typically include the *numina* (*gzhi bdag*), headmen, villagers, 'spirit-helpers', trance mediums, divination masters and sometimes Tibetan doctors and Lamas. It is evident from field research (Studley, 2014) in northwest Yunnan that most human actors attempt to interact with *numina* on the basis of contractual reciprocity in return for patronage, governance, protection and blessing.

The *gzhi bdag* make most of the decisions in terms of what constitutes acceptable behaviour, if a new intervention constitutes a 'disturbance', if honouring and appeasement is adequate, if restitution is apposite, if the domain and biophysical resources are being adequately protected, if trespassing has occurred, and if grazing and the collection of minor forest products is within acceptable limits. The human participants engage in ritual enquiry with the help of a trance medium or divination specialist (Figure 7.9) in response to a vision, trance, omen, theophany or calamity in order to decide if *numina* are upset with them, if so which *numina*, what offence has been committed and what types of restitution are required.

Although *gzhi bdag* are autocratic in terms of governance they are dependent upon human agency to re-enspirit their domain by engaging in invocation rituals and liturgies (*bsang yig*). Re-enspiriting minimally occurs at least on an annual basis by the community, and *gzhi bdag* must be invoked by name and their terrestrial abode re-designated and re-inscribed geospatially through ritual demarcation (Coggins and Zeren, 2014). If not, the *gzhi bdag* will become displaced and de-territorialised and lose their power, status, authority and patronage (Ramble, 2008).

Figure 7.9 Divination using a sheep's scapula on a fire
(Permission from Dr Erdenatuya Urtnast (pending))

7.8.9.2 Sui generis *governance*

Some villages have set up voluntary *ad hoc* patrols, traditionally known as *ri bsher*, on the basis of *sui generis* norms to prevent outsiders or hunters from trespassing on the domain of their *gzhi bdag* or disturbing them (Studley, 2014).

7.8.9.3 *Monastic governance*

Tibetan Buddhist/Bon institutions only "maintain local regulations" (Shen et al., 2015: 1523) in the environs of monasteries or on the 'tamed' pilgrimage mountains they have co-opted. They have no jurisdiction over enspirited SNS that are characterised, for lay people, by the ontic modalities of being, participation and belonging (Eliade, 1959), which are all alien concepts for Bon and TB.

7.8.9.4 ri rgya *governance*

Sealed enclosures, or *ri rgya* (Figure 7.10), which often ensure the double protection of SNS, are the result of a formal ritual presided over by lamas

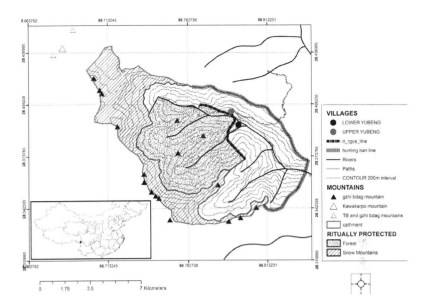

Figure 7.10 A ri rgya line (broad dashes) in the Yubeng Valley demarcates protected SNS from the human domain

(Studley, 2014)

and village headmen. Although they are widespread, they are very localised and unknown in much of southwest China (Studley, 2014).

Notes

1 The Yangtze, Mekong, Salween and Brahmaputra.
2 Based on Stalin's (1951) definition of nationality.
3 Tibetans who live in Eastern Tibet and speak Kham or one of its dialects as their mother tongue.
4 Of northwest Yunnan.
5 Predicated on constant sum scaling.
6 These were sent home during the Cultural Revolution and gave up their vows, but still perform local household ceremonies, mostly associated with rites of passage.
7 DBH = diameter at breast height (at 1.3m) – is a standard method of expressing the diameter of the trunk or bole of a standing tree.
8 Basal area is the common term used to describe the average amount of an area occupied by tree stems. It is defined as the total cross-sectional area of all stems in a stand measured at breast height, and expressed as per unit of land area (typically square metres per hectare).

 9 According to Jinba (2013) it is 77%.
10 Tonpa Shenrab (*ston pa gshen rab*) of Tagzig (Iran) is the founder of the Bon tradition of Tibet.
11 Guru Rinpoche (*gu ru rin po che*) or Padmasambhava (*pad ma 'byung gnas*) is the founder of Tibetan Buddhism.
12 GIS calculation by author.
13 Constant sum scaling is a technique where respondents are asked to allocate a constant sum of units among the stimulus objects according to some specified criterion.

8 The challenge of perpetuating SNS

8.1 Institutional support for SNS

SNS require institutional support because their biocultural integrity is being undermined, but paradoxically the undermining includes some unintended consequences by conservation organisations (IUCN and ICCA).

Not only do enspirited SNS appear to lack recognition under IUCN governance designations, but IUCN appears to be undermining them and the livelihood and culture of the people who protect them. In 2017, for example, they nominated a large nature reserve[1] for World Heritage status (WHS) that has historically been nurtured by nomads as seasonal pasture from at least the 19th century according to Western travellers[2] and probably for millennia. It proceeded with the nomination in a country with a track record of what has been called 'cultural genocide' (ICJ, 1960: 117; UNDRIP, 1994: Art. 7, 2007: Art. 8), particularly among nomads since 1998, under the aegis of what is euphemistically known as "ecological migration" (Foggin, 2008: 27). They nominated the "property" only under a "natural criteria" in spite of the fact that they recognised that "there are tangible and intangible cultural attributes . . . including sacred mountains and sites, of local and national significance" (IUCN, 2017: 31), there are "intangible values embedded in the landscape", the local pastoralists play a significant role in stewardship (IUCN, 2017: 37) and their Indigenous knowledge contributes to biodiversity (Miller, 2008). Furthermore they appeared to override UNDRIP resolution 4.048 on Indigenous peoples by failing to consider that the national policy of the state party since 1998 has been to "end the nomadic way of life for all herders" (Qi, 1998), there is evidence (prior to the bid) of forced resettlement (Kernan, 2013) and 153 cases of self-immolation in the neighbouring region (one in the property),[3] they knew that the property was not *terra nullius* as claimed by the state party as there is evidence of permanent habitation dating back to the early Holocene (Meyer et al., 2017; MHURD, 2016), and they proceeded with the nomination in the knowledge that local people had "expressed real concern about relocation" (IUCN, 2017: 35). The state party told IUCN that "no forced relocation or exclusion of the traditional users of the property will be undertaken or pursued" (IUCN, 2017: 40), and they assured UNESCO that they would "fully respect the will of the local herders and their traditional culture, religious beliefs, and lifestyle" (Myers, 2017). Only time will tell if these commitments are honoured!

Indigenous Conserved Territories and Community Conserved Areas (ICCAs) is a new IUCN governance category with less history and track record than WHS, that recognises the *de jure* or *de facto* authority of local communities to manage protected areas that have cultural, spiritual and utilitarian significance for them, and in this it represented a step forward. The challenge that ICCA seeks to address is that sacred natural sites and spiritual governance have not been explicitly included in the governance matrix of protected areas (Borrini-Feyerabend et al., 2014). The ICCA approach is predicated on human agency and "its margins are riddled with hotspots where control over land and resources is disputed, and the legitimacy of lifestyles and livelihoods challenged" (Martin, 2012: 62). Furthermore, there are dangers that its conservation approach may destroy the endogenous processes that generate biocultural diversity (Apgar et al., 2011). ICCA certification was expected to show conservation benefits according to conventional criteria, but it has often entangled communities in a web of international and national law and policy that threatened to impose exclusionary and preservationist measures under the guise of community conservation.

8.2   Matching Indigenous beliefs with modern jurisprudence

'Juristic personhood' appears to offer an alternative to the IUCN's more traditional approaches to the conservation of nature (Studley and Bleisch, 2018). Both anthropologists and lawyers recognise that there are major differences and tensions between Indigenous beliefs and modern jurisprudence and have suggested alternatives in various forms of 'juristic personhood'. Bohannan (1957) has suggested that 'juristic' entities should be locally defined rather than by the court or government, and Petrazycki (2011: 189–190) has suggested "legal relationships with animated entities", which resonates with Animistic relational ontologies. Given the complexities and disparate nature of local definitions and norms, it might be easier for enspirited SNS to be "integrated into the circle of 'legal subjects' in order to survive" (Stavru, 2016: online) and for the concept of juristic personhood to be infused with Indigenous meaning (Cajete, 2000).

Clearly, more research is required in order to address legal systems that do not appear to be fit for purpose, and under the aegis of legal pluralism and a *sui generis* framework, to identify legal systems predicated on ethno-jurisprudence and customary law.

8.3　Congruence with Animism

The concept of juristic personhood resonates with the beliefs underpinning most sacred natural sites. SNS are typically enspirited by a unique geospecific spirit with a unique personhood capable of spiritual governance. This is predicated on a pluriversal Animistic tradition which does not resonate well with ecocentrism, panentheism or pantheism.

Ecocentrism is monistic, and the concept of rights is a construction from outside an Indigenous Animistic context (Solon, 2014).

Panentheism assumes an intrinsic connection between all living things and the physical world and focuses on gnostic mystic advancement in order to merge with the world soul, which is an alien approach for Animists.

Although pantheism is popular in some conservation circles (Harrison, 2004), it does not recognise deities who are personal and anthropogenic. The approach robs particular life forms of their own measure of significance and agency (Plumwood, 1993) and discounts "the particularity of place and ecosystem and the diversity of life" (Northcott, 1996: 113).

8.4　Legal acceptance

Colonial judges in India (*Mullick v Mullick*, 1925) were able to employ "the great legal freedom to personify, almost it would seem on a whim" (Naffine, 2009: 166), allowing them to infer juristic personhood on an idol and operating on the assumption that an enspirited idol certainly had legal standing. The colonial judges employed a line of reasoning that mirrors a key element of the argument in favour of legal standing for other-than-human persons; the directly affected parties deserve the courts' consideration of their interests, and may also require the courts to appoint appropriate legal representatives to argue their case for them (Totten, 2015). In this context, it appears perverse that judicial decisions in North America have failed to address juristic personhood issues. In *Sierra Club v. Morton* (1972), the justices could only inquire about standing for threatened natural resources; in *Reece v. Edmonton City* (2011), the Alberta courts would not allow animal advocates to speak on behalf of an old elephant that was suffering in a zoo; and the Canadian Supreme Court (*Ktunaxa Nation v. BC*, 2017) made no attempt to ensure that the Grizzly Bear Spirit was represented in their deliberations about the impact of a proposed ski resort on Qat'muk, a place of spiritual significance for the Ktunaxa Nation.

Critics (Laidlaw, 2017) have responded to the Canadian Supreme Court ruling by positing a number of important comments that have wider application. They suggest a lack of 'due process', with reference to other similar cases on the basis of comity of nations because the court did not:

1   ensure that the Grizzly Bear Spirit was represented by a guardian in court
(*Mullick v. Mullick*, 1925; *Hou v. BLNR*, 2015)

2   invite a *Ktunaxa* shaman (or similar person) as an expert witness who could express the response of the Grizzly Bear Spirit to the ski resort
(*Hou v. BLNR*, 2015)

3   consider granting juristic personhood to the *Qut'muk* area[4]
4   consider the United Nation Declaration of the Rights of Indigenous People
(UNDRIP, 2007)

Some scholars have suggested that extensive legislative change will be necessary to recognise legal standing for other-than-human persons. A case such as *Reece v. Edmonton City* (2011), however, suggests that it is already within the power of the judiciary to consider these issues. As Chief Justice Fraser (dissenting) asserted, unusual cases such as *Reece* offer a fertile ground for the growth of law in a changing society. It appears that the judiciary already has at its disposal the legal tools necessary to accommodate standing for SNS and protected areas, and judges need only to make use of them (Totten, 2015).

There appears to be no reason why 'juristic personhood' cannot be used as part of a legal regime to ensure standing for protected areas (Sobrevila, 2008) and particularly for enspirited SNS. If *numina* or SNS are granted legal status as juristic persons they have standing as a plaintiff. If their biocultural integrity is compromised (if, for example, an SNS is threatened with clear-felling), then they can seek redress in court through a guardian, and the burden of proof lies with the offending party/parties.

8.5   The question of guardians

Although juristic persons have standing, they are also perpetual minors and require guardians to represent their interests (especially in court). In the context of SNS, the most suitable guardians would be answerable to a local "community of believers" (Marsilius of Padua in Emerton, 2015: 72). In his *Defensor pacis* (written in 1324), Marsilius embraced a form of democracy that views the people, or the 'community of believers', as the only legitimate source of political authority. He argues that sovereignty lies with the people and that citizens should elect, correct and, if necessary, depose its political leaders. In more recent times, Nisbet (2014) has argued that the authority of the community is essential for accountable and legitimate local decision-making.

In the context of Tibetan SNS, for example, appropriate guardians might be the hereditary village leader, a trance medium, or a divination master who can establish the wishes and demands of the *numina*.

In a Hawaiian court case (*MKAH v. BLNR*, 2013), a descendant of the *Kanaka Maoli* (native Hawaiians) wrote an affidavit (accepted by the court) that granted him the power of attorney to act and speak on behalf of a spirit named *Mo'oinanea* that inhabits Mount Mauna Kea.

There are a number of judicial options if minors are not represented. Under the aegis of western jurisprudence, judges are able to appoint, by court order, a guardian ad litum for the duration of the legal action or a state guardian *parens patriae* on a longer-term basis.

8.6   Scaling-up

Most enspirited SNS are small, such as those in southwest China, which typically average 250ha (Studley, 2014) and are therefore ritually protected by a small group of local people, which could represent the SNS in court. Challenges arise, however, in terms of standing for larger natural entities such as the Great Barrier Reef or the Mekong River. The Great Barrier Reef, an important cultural site for many Aboriginal and Torres Strait Islander peoples, is being degraded as a result of global carbon emissions and inland development (Marshall and Johnson, 2007), but who will represent it in court and who can be sued? The Mekong is especially sacred to Buddhist and Animistic communities who live along its banks in the nations through which it flows. It presents different problems because it crosses multiple borders and jurisdictions. As a result, appointing guardian(s) would require transnational regional cooperation, and enforcement would require several countries working together with several sets of national legislation.

8.7   Establishing priorities

Given the current threatened status of SNS in many parts of the world and their lack of recognition, it would appear that the granting of juristic person-hood to those SNS that are outside of PAs is more of a priority than those already under the aegis of conservation designations. Furthermore, juris-tic personhood is augmented by customary laws, *sui generis* frameworks and ritual protection of SNS that are often extant in Indigenous societies. Although as a legal term 'juristic personhood' or its cross-cultural equiva-lent does not exist in lay Tibetan and may not appear in the lexicons of many

Indigenous people, as a concept it resonates with Animist worldviews and ontologies (Studley, 2014).

Although SNS occur in all IUCN categories of protected area (Dudley, 2008), it is apparent that their extent, distribution and spiritual governance is largely unknown, and even less is known about SNS in the homelands of Indigenous people (Studley, 2014). It is vitally important, especially when establishing or expanding protected areas, to identify and map SNS and to record the expectations of the *numina* who inhabit the SNS and any customary laws that might affect conservation outcomes, positively or negatively.

8.8　Ensuring standing for nature spirits (or environmental spirits)

Although Indigenous people have engaged in 'legal relationships' and 'contractual reciprocity' with 'nature spirits' or 'environmental spirits' since time immemorial and legal precedents have been set, the standing of environmental spirits who inhabit landscape features remains ambiguous. It appears as if Indigenous legal practices by definition will have to remain subordinate to the knowledge-and-power systems of 'western jurisprudence'. However, even through this lens, juristic personhood may offer a way for Indigenous people to engage with the dominant legal system.

To reiterate from Chapter 4, colonial judges established a precedent (*Mullick v. Mullick*, 1925) for granting juristic personhood to the spirits (or gods) who enspirited idols and temples, contingent upon an enspiriting ceremony, and applying Salmond's definition and explanation of the capabilities of 'persons':

> So far as legal theory is concerned, a person is any being whom the law (or society) regards as capable of 'rights and duties'. Any being that is so capable is a person, whether a human being or not, and no being that is not so capable is a person even though he be a man.
>
> (Salmond, 1913: 82)

On this basis, colonial judges recognised that an enspirited idol was a juristic person with standing, and they appointed a guardian to represent the enspirited idol.

Furthermore, the practice is not some anachronistic colonial legacy; Indian judges continue to regard spirits/gods as juristic persons with standing (*Akhara v Lord Ram*, 2010), as do British judges (*Bumper v. Met. Police*, 1991), where in a dispute about ownership of an idol from an Indian temple site, the object was deemed to be a claimant.

Under the rubric of 'legal relationships' rather than 'juristic personhood' and 'personal character' rather than 'person', Petrazycki (2011: 87) argues that:

the subject of legal relationships obligations, and rights, can correspond to all possible representations of a personal character. These can be objects that are not actually alive but are represented as animate (such as stones, plants, and so forth), animals and their spirits, persons (including their embryos and their spirits after death), human societies and institutions, and various deities and other incorporeal spirits.

Notwithstanding the legal precedent, both Stone's seminal article (*Should Trees Have Standing?*, 1972) and the provision of 'nature rights' in the constitution of Ecuador and Bolivia (Shelton, 2015) provided a platform that allowed jurists/legislators the freedom to extend the concept of juristic personhood to ecosystems (rivers, mountains, catchments). But it is questionable if conceptually it is limited to the biophysical world.

Significantly, most of the recent ecosystems that have been declared as juristic persons include landscape features that are enspirited, and all are located in the homelands of people with a foundational Animistic worldview, including Hinduism given its tribal Animistic foundation (Tiwari, 2002).

Perversely, although reference is made to the spirits or gods who enspirit or embody ecosystems (the *kaitiaki* in New Zealand and *Ganga Ma* in India), there is no explicit reference to their juristic personhood. It still appears to be largely "unthinkable" (Stone, 1972: 450) to apply the term specifically to 'nature spirits' or genius loci (the spirits or *numina* that inhabit specific landscapes) in most jurisdictions.

To date, there has only been one case (*KAHEA v. UHH*, 2013) where the courts allowed a spirit (one that inhabits Mount Mauna Kea, Hawaii) to be represented. Although a shaman was allowed to testify as an expert witness on behalf of a spirit (Rios, 2016), the court would not grant standing to the spirit.

It is crucial to note that as far as many Indigenous societies are concerned, the *numina* that inhabit their SNS "are capable of rights and duties" and engage in spiritual governance and should qualify as juristic persons.

Notes

1 Known as *koko-shili* in Mongolian (*koko* = blue and *shili* = grass-covered mountains).
2 Hedin, Prjevalsky, Rijnhart, Rockhill and Wellby mention seeing thousands of yak while passing through Koko Shili.
3 Tenzin Sherab on 27/5/2013.
4 The Whanganui, Ganges and Atrato catchments have been granted juristic person status with standing in early 2017.

9 How can sacred natural sites best be prosecuted?

The successful prosecution of enspirited sacred natural sites for conservation goals and biocultural enhancement is contingent upon a number of factors. These factors include a pluriversal legal framework, a polycentric worldview, institutional support, advocacy and judicial traction, an intercultural approach, and the optimisation (within conservation planning) of local lay support for the ritual protection of SNS.

A precedent has been set (outlined in Chapters 4–6) for courts and legislatures to embrace a pluriversal legal framework when safeguarding nature. The recent legislation has provided conservationists and Indigenous people with new legal tools (nature rights) and legal regimes (juristic personhood and spiritual governance) to safeguard SNS and ecosystems. There is no reason why juristic personhood and nature rights cannot both be used to safeguard protected areas and OECMs (other effective area-based conservation measures) including ICCAs and ISNS, especially given the use of the latter in litigation. It appears that the judiciary already has at its disposal the legal tools necessary to accommodate standing for ISNS and protected areas, and judges need only to make use of them.

In order to enhance the biocultural diversity of ISNS, it is important to bridge the gap between the universal worldview of most conservation planners and the Animistic worldview of most Indigenous peoples who nurture most of the world's SNS. Polycentric worldviews need to be embraced because they create space for the acceptance of multiple worlds, invoking alternative epistemologies (ways of knowing) and ontologies (ways of being) in different worlds. Pluriversality is already being harnessed by Indigenous groups to re-work conservation ideas and practice (de la Cadena, 2010).

To date, some 'conservation' institutions (IUCN, ICCA, WHC and UNESCO) have (wittingly or unwittingly) undermined enspirited SNS, pathologised Indigenous people and failed to recognise spiritual agency or endogenous processes. There is an urgent need for institutional support in order to update the IUCN governance matrix so that both SNS and spiritual governance are embraced, re-map protected and conserved areas so that SNS are included (and local norms respected), retrospectively re-designate UNESCO (MAB reserves and World Heritage Sites) and ASEAN heritage parks and EuroNatura initiatives, and recognise local people and nomads as part of the solution, not just an obstacle.

In order for the juristic personhood of sacred natural sites (and their resident *numina*) to become normative, there is a need for advocacy groups (such as Community Environmental Legal Defence Fund or Natural Justice) or environmental lawyers to help Indigenous people with test cases to secure standing for threatened SNS. Hopefully, this will lead to judicial traction, resulting in a critical mass where courts increasingly find in favour of other-than-human entities that are threatened.

Lay participation in ritual protection of enspirited SNS has not been fully recognised in much of the widely quoted literature or in conservation planning to date. It is important that all the stakeholders are involved in conservation planning, but the parties often adhere to very disparate knowledge systems, and there is no cross-cultural conceptual or supra-cultural framework for epistemological integration. In order to ensure the full participation of lay people in environmental protection, an intercultural approach is suggested predicated on synergistic bridging and knowledge-brokerage. The aim of knowledge-brokerage is to bring multiple worldviews together around the aspirations and challenges of local lay people. The purpose being to expose elements or interventions that are incompatible with the aspirations, worldviews and life-ways of local lay people and to identify areas of mutual synergy.

In conclusion, local lay people should be able to negotiate and engage in the terms of SNS protection themselves in order to perpetuate a unique landscape and tradition they have maintained for millennia.

References

ABColombia (2017) *Colombian Constitutional Court Sets a Global Precedent.* London: ABColombia.

ACHPR African Commission on Human and Peoples' Rights (2017) *Final Communiqué of the 60th Ordinary Session of the African Commission on Human and Peoples' Rights / 60th Ordinary Session/ACHPR.* [online] available from <www.achpr.org/sessions/60th/info/communique60/> [11 July 2017].

African Biodiversity Network (ABN) (2016) *A Call for Legal Recognition of Sacred Natural Sites and Territories, and Their Customary Governance Systems: Submission to African Commission.* available from <http://africanbiodiversity.org/downloads/1056/>.

Ah Xiang (1998) *Political, Social, Cultural, Historical Analysis Of China: Homepage.* [online] available from <www.republicanchina.org/homepage.html> [8 September 2015].

Akhara v. Lord Ram (2010) *Nirmohi Akhara v. Baboo Priya Dutt Ram (FB) 2010(3) A.R.C. 708: 2010(61) R.C.R.(Civil) 650.* Allahabad High Court (Lucknow Bench).

Allard, C. and Skogvang, A.P.S.F. (2015) *Indigenous Rights in Scandinavia: Autonomous Sami Law* [online]. Farnham: Ashgate Publishing, Ltd.

Allendorf, T.D., Brandt, J.S., and Yang, J.M. (2014) 'Local Perceptions of Tibetan Village Sacred Forests in Northwest Yunnan'. *Biological Conservation* 169, 303–310.

The American Bison Society (2016) *American Bison Society: Buffalo Treaty 2nd Anniversary.* [online] available from <www.ambisonsociety.org/Buffalo-Treaty-2nd-Anniversary.aspx> [26 November 2016].

Anderson, D., Salick, J., Moseley, B., and Xiaokun, O. (2005) 'Conserving the Sacred Medicine Mountains: A Vegetation Analysis of Tibetan Sacred Sites in Northwest Yunnan'. *Biodiversity and Conservation* 14, 3065–3091.

Apgar, J., Ataria, J., and Allene, W. (2011) 'Managing beyond Designation: Supporting Endogenous Processes for Nurturing Biocultural Development'. *International Journal of Heritage Studies* 17 (6), 555–570.

Asher, M. (1979) *Ancient Energy: Key to the Universe.* New York: Harper & Row.

Awang Jikmed (2014) *Role of Tibetan Sacred Natural Sites in Conservation: Understanding Tibetan Attitudes toward Sacred Natural Sites in the Gador Jowo Sacred Mountains, in the Sanjiangyuan National Nature Reserve.* Masters Dissertation. Canterbury: University of Kent.

Babcock, H.M. (2016) 'A Brook with Legal Rights: The Rights of Nature in Court'. *Ecology LQ* 43, 1.

Bacigalupo, A.M. (2010) *Shamans of the Foye Tree: Gender, Power, and Healing among Chilean Mapuche*. Austin: University of Texas Press.

Baksh, R. and Harcourt, W. (2015) *The Oxford Handbook of Transnational Feminist Movements*. Oxford: Oxford Handbooks.

Bell, T. (1992) *The Jurisprudence of Polycentric Law*. Chicago: Chicago School of Law.

Bellezza, J.V. (2005) *Spirit-Mediums, Sacred Mountains and Related Bon Textual Traditions in Upper Tibet*. Leiden: Brill.

Bellezza, J.V. (1997) *Divine Dyads, Ancient Civilization in Tibet*. Dharamsala, India: Library of Tibetan Works & Archives.

Berry, T. (1999) *The Great Work: Our Way to the Future*. New York: Bell Tower.

Berry, T. (1988) *The Dream of the Earth*. San Francisco: Sierra Club Books.

Berzin, A. (2013) *A Survey of Tibetan History: Reading Notes Taken by Alexander Berzin from Tsepon, W. D. Shakabpa, Tibet: A Political History*. New Haven, CT: Yale University Press.

Bhagwat, S. and Palmer, M. (2009) 'Conservation: The World's Religions Can Help'. *Nature* 461 (7260), 37.

Bird-David, N. (1999) '"Animism" Revisited: Personhood, Environment, and Relational Epistemology 1'. *Current Anthropology* 40 (S1), S67–S91.

Blanc, M. and Tovey, H. (2017) *Food, Nature and Society: Rural Life in Late Modernity*. Abingdon: Taylor & Francis.

Blaser, M. (2010) *Storytelling Globalization from the Chaco and Beyond*. Durham: Duke University Press.

Bleisch, B. and Wong, H. (1990) *Global Markets and Sacred Mountains: Nature Conservation in the Tibetan Areas of Sichuan and Gansu Provinces*. Hong Kong: China Exploration and Research Society.

Blondeau, A.-M. and Steinkellner, E. (1998) *Tibetan Mountain Deities: Their Cults and Representations: Papers Presented at a Panel of the 7th Seminar of the International Association for Tibetan Studies-Graz 1995*. Wien: Verlag der Osterreichischen Akademie der Wissenschaften.

Bohannan, P. (1957) *Judgement and Justice among the Tiv*. Oxford: International African Institute by Oxford University Press.

Bollier, D. (2007) 'The Growth of the Commons Paradigm'. in *Understanding Knowledge as a Commons*. ed. by Hess, C. and Ostrom, E. Cambridge: The MIT Press, 27–40.

Borrini-Feyerabend, G.B.R., Hay-Edie, T., Lang, B., Rastogi, A., and Sandwith, T. (2014) *A Primer on Governance for Protected and Conserved Areas, Stream on Enhancing Diversity and Quality of Governance*. Gland, Switzerland: IUCN World Parks Congress.

Borrini-Feyerabend, G.B.R. and Hill, R. (2015) 'Governance for the Conservation of Nature'. *Protected Area Governance and Management* 169–206.

Bowker, J. (2000) *The Concise Oxford Dictionary of World Religions*. Oxford: Oxford University Press.

Braidotti, R. (2013) *The Posthuman*. Hoboken: Wiley.

Brautigam, N. (2011) *Above the Mukpa: The Shifting Ground of Khumbu's Sacred Geography*. [online] available from <http://digitalcollections.sit.edu/isp_collection/1234/> [29 December 2015].

Buckley, L. (2007) *Tibetan Sacred Lands: A Values-Based Approach to Conservation*. Washington, DC: Worldwatch Institute.

Buddhadasa, B. (1986) *Dharmic Socialism* (Translated by E. Swearer). Bangkok: Interreligious Commission for Development.

Bum, T. (2016) 'The Changing Roles of Tibetan Mountain Deities in the Context of Emerging Environmental Issues: Dkar Po Lha Bsham in Yul Shul'. *Asian Highland Perspectives* 40, 1–33.

Bumper v Met. Police (1991) *Bumper Development Corporation v Commissioner of Police of The Metropolis and Others [1991] EWCA Civ J0213–5, [1991] 1 WLR 1362*. London: Court of Appeal.

Cai Hua (2001) *A Society without Fathers or Husbands: The Na of China*. New York: Zone Books.

Cajete, G. (2000) *Native Science: Natural Laws of Interdependence, Ceremony, Body Sense*. Santa Fe New Mexico: Clear Light Publishers.

Callicott, J. (1989) *In Defence of the Land Ethic*. Albany: State University of New York Press.

Cano Pecharroman, L. (2018) 'Rights of Nature: Rivers That Can Stand in Court'. *Resources* 7 (1), 13.

Capra, F. and Mattei, U. (2015) *The Ecology of Law: Toward a Legal System in Tune with Nature and Community*. Oakland: Berrett-Koehler Publishers.

Carlisle, K. and Gruby, R.L. (2017) 'Polycentric Systems of Governance: A Theoretical Model for the Commons'. [online] *Policy Studies Journal* https://onlinelibrary.wiley.com/doi/full/10.1111/psj.12212 [16 Sept 2018].

Carlson, B. (2017) 'Why Are Indigenous People Such Avid Users of Social Media?'. [online] *The Guardian* https://www.theguardian.com/commentisfree/2017/apr/27/whyareindigenouspeoplesuchavidusersofsocialmedia [16 Sept 2018].

Chapin, M. (1991) 'Losing the Way of the Great Father'. *New Scientist* 131 (1781), 40–44.

Charman, K. (2008) 'Ecuador First to Grant Nature Constitutional Rights'. *Capitalism Nature Socialism* 19 (4), 131–132.

Chuwa, L. (2014) *African Indigenous Ethics in Global Bioethics: Interpreting Ubuntu* [online] vol. 1. New York City: Springer.

Clarke, B. and Rossini, M. (2016) 'Posthuman Themes'. in *The Cambridge Companion to Literature and the Posthuman*. Cambridge Companions to Literature. Cambridge: Cambridge University Press, 139–208.

Coggins, C. and Hutchinson, T. (2006) 'The Political Ecology of Geopiety: Nature Conservation in Tibetan Communities of Northwest Yunnan'. *Asian Geographer* 25 (1–2), 85–107.

Coggins, C. and Zeren, G. (2014) 'Animate Landscapes: Nature Conservation and the Production of Agropastoral Sacred Space in Shangrila'. in *Mapping Shangrila: Contested Landscapes in the Sino-Tibetan Borderlands*. ed. by Coggins, C. and Yeh, E.T. Seattle: University of Washington Press, 205–228.

Cohen, R.S. and Tauber, A.I. (2013) *Philosophies of Nature: The Human Dimension: In Celebration of Erazim Kohák*. vol. 195. Berlin: Springer Science.

Colding, J. and Folke, C. (2001) 'Social Taboos, "Invisible" Systems of Local Resource Management and Biological Conservation'. *Ecological Applications* 1 (2), 584–600.

Combe, G. (1926) *A Tibetan on Tibet*. London: T Fisher Unwin Ltd.

Couch, K.I. (2010) 'Atonement: Californian Tribe Dances for Salmon in Aotearoa'. *Tekaraka* 47 (Winter), 14–19.

CRIC (undated) *Universidad Autónoma Indígena Intercultural UAII | Consejo Regional Indígena Del Cauca: CRIC*. [online] available from <www.cric-colombia.org/portal/universidad-autonoma-indigena-intercultural-uaii/> [10 June 2017].

Cullinan, C. (2011) *Wild Law: A Manifesto for Earth Justice*. 2nd Edition. Totnes, UK: Green Books.

Dakpa, N. (2006) *Opening the Door to Bon*. Boulder, CO: Snow Lion Publications.

Daly, E. (2012) 'The Ecuadorian Exemplar: The First Ever Vindications of Constitutional Rights of Nature'. *Review of European Community & International Environmental Law* 21 (1), 63–66.

Daniel, V.E. (1996) *Charred Lullabies: Chapters in an Anthropography of Violence*. Princeton: Princeton University Press.

Darlington, S. (2000) 'Rethinking Buddhism & Development: The Emergence of Environmentalist Monks in Thailand'. *Journal of Buddhist Ethics* 7, 1–17.

Davidson-Hunt, I. and Berkes, F. (2003) 'Learning as You Journey: Anishinaabe Perception of Social-Ecological Environments and Adaptive Learning'. *Ecology and Society* 8 (1), 5.

Day, J. (2013) *Making Senses of the Past: Toward a Sensory Archaeology*. Carbondale: SIU Press.

De Castro, E.V. (1992) *From the Enemy's Point of View: Humanity and Divinity in an Amazonian Society*. Chicago: University of Chicago Press.

De la Cadena, M. (2010) Indigenous Cosmopolitics in The Andes: Conceptual Reflections beyond "Politics" https://anthrosource.onlinelibrary.wiley.com/doi/pdf/10.1111/j.1548-1360.2010.01061.x

Deloria, V. (1999) 'Knowing and Understanding: Traditional Education in the Modern World'. in *Spirit & Reason: The Vine Deloria, Jr., Reader* [online]. ed. by Deloria, B. and Foehner, K. Golden: Fulcrum Publishing, 137–143.

Derks, S. (2009) *Power and Pilgrimage: Dealing with Class, Gender and Ethnic Inequality at a Bolivian Marian Shrine*. vol. 47. Munster: LIT Verlag Münster.

De Sales, A. (2001) 'The Go-between: Reflections on a Mechanism of Ritual Exchange'. in *Expanding the Economic Concept of Exchange*. ed. by Gerschlager, C. New York City: Springer, 121–132.

De Sales, A. (2011) Time, Identity and Historical Change in the Hills of Nepal, *European Bulletin of Himalayan Research, 39*.

Dongyal, K.T. (2008) *Light of Fearless Indestructible Wisdom: The Life and Legacy of HH Dudjom Rinpoche*. Boulder, CO: Snow Lion Publications.

Dudley, N. (2008) *Guidelines for Applying Protected Area Management Categories*. Gland, Switzerland: IUCN.

Dudley, N., Higgins-Zogib, L., and Mansourian, S. (2009) 'The Links between Protected Areas, Faiths, and Sacred Natural Sites'. *Conservation Biology* 23 (3), 568–577.

Eberhard, C. (2014) *Culture, Community, Comparison: Approaching Law in the Pluriverse*. Farnham: Ashgate Publishing, Ltd.

Eckel, M. (1998) 'Is There a Buddhist Philosophy of Nature?'. in *Philosophies of Nature: The Human Dimension*. ed. by Cohen, R. and Tauber, A. Dordrecht: Kluwer, 53–69.

The Ecologist (2016) 'Greens Commit to Rights of Nature Law'. *The Ecologist* [online].

Ecuador National Assembly (2008) *Ecuador: 2008 Constitution in English*. [online] available from <http://pdba.georgetown.edu/Constitutions/Ecuador/english08.html> [12 April 2017].

Eliade, M. (1959) *The Sacred and the Profane: The Nature of Religion*. Boston: Houghton Mifflin Harcourt.

Emerton, E. (2015) *The Defensor Pacis of Marsiglio of Padua: A Critical Study*. Chapel Hill: FB&C.

Epstein, L. (2002) *Khams Pa Histories: Visions of People Place and Authority: Piats 2000 Tibetan Studies Proceedings of the Ninth Seminar of the International Association for Tibetan Studies Seminar International Association for Tibetan Studies*. Leiden & Boston: Brill.

Ermakov, D. (2008) *Bø and Bön: Ancient Shamanic Traditions of Siberia and Tibet in Their Relation to the Teachings of a Central Asian Buddha*. [online] available from <http://philpapers.org/rec/ERMBAB> [12 December 2016].

Escobar, A. (2015) 'Commons in the Pluriverse'. in *Patterns of Commoning*. ed. by Bollier, D. and Helfrich, S. Amherst, MA: Commons Strategy Group and Off the Common Press, 348–360.

Escobar, A. (2008) *Territories of Difference: Place, Movements, Life*. Durham: Duke University Press.

Fausto, C. (2008) 'Too Many Owners: Mastery and Ownership in Amazonia'. *Mana* 14 (2), 329–366.

Feng Youzhi (1992) *Xikang Shi Shi Yi (Supplementary Collections of Xikang History)*. Kangding: Cultural-Historical Data Committee.

Flores, E.K. (2011) *Petition to the State of Hawaii Board of Land and Natural Resources Requesting the Participation of Mo'oinanea in the Proceedings*. [online] available from <https://dlnr.hawaii.gov/mk/files/2016/10/Ex.-A-028.pdf> [1 June 2018].

Foggin, J.M. (2008) 'Depopulating the Tibetan Grasslands: National Policies and Perspectives for the Future of Tibetan Herders in Qinghai Province, China'. *Mountain Research and Development* 28 (1), 26–31.

Fowler, H.N. (1921) *Plato in Twelve Volumes*. vol. 12. Cambridge, MA & London: Harvard University Press & William Heinemann Ltd.

Frazer, S.J. (1890) *The Golden Bough*. Ware: Wordsworth Editions Ltd.

Fuller, L. (1969) *The Morality of Law*. New Haven, CT: Yale University Press.

Gadgil, M. and Vartak, V.D. (1976) 'The Sacred Groves of Western Ghats in India'. *Economic Botany* 30 (2), 152–160.

Geisler, N. and Watkins, W.D. (2003) *Worlds Apart: A Handbook on World Views*. Eugene: WIPF and Stock Publishers.

Goldstein, M. (1997) *The Snow Lion and the Dragon: China Tibet and the Dalai Lama*. London: University of California Press.

Goldstein, M. and Kapstein, M. (1998) *Buddhism in Contemporary Tibet: Religious Revival and Cultural Identity*. New Delhi: Motilal Banarsidass Publishers.

Grant Township (2014) *Grant Township, Indiana County, Community Bill of Rights Ordinance.* Grant Township. https://www.foodandwaterwatch.org/sites/default/ files/frack_actions_granttownshipindianacountypa.pdf

Grzeszczak, R. and Karolewski, I.P. (2012) *The Multi-Level and Polycentric European Union: Legal and Political Studies.* vol. 69. Munster: LIT Verlag Münster.

Guha, R. (2000) 'The Malign Encounter: The Chipko Movement and Competing Visions of Nature'. in *Who Will Save the Forests.* ed. by Banuri, T. and Marglin, F. London: Zed Books, 80–113.

Hall, G. and Hendricks, J. (2013) *Dreaming a New Earth: Raimon Panikkar and Indigenous Spiritualities.* Eugene: WIPF and Stock Publishers.

Hallowell, A.I. (2002) 'Ojibwa Ontology, Behavior, and World View'. in *Readings in Indigenous Religions.* ed. by Harvey, G. vol. 22. London & New York: Bloomsbury Publishing, 17–49.

Hallowell, A.I. (1992) *The Ojibwa of Berens River, Manitoba: Ethnography into History.* Fort Worth & Toronto: Harcourt Brace Jovanovich College Publishers.

Hallowell, A.I. (1960) 'Ojibwa Ontology, Behavior and World View'. in *Culture in History: Essays in Honor of Paul Radin.* ed. by Diamond, S. New York: Columbia University Press, 1–25.

Handa, O.C. (2001) *Buddhist Western Himalaya: Part I. A Politico-Religious History.* New Delhi: Indus Publishing Company.

Harding, S. (2006) *Animate Earth: Science, Intuition, and Gaia.* Hartford: Chelsea Green Publishing.

Hardison, P. (2006) *Indigenous Peoples and the Commons.* On the Commons [online]. http://www.onthecommons.org/indigenous-peoples-and-commons#sthash. tavyofPk.dpbs

Harrell, S. (ed.) (2001) *Perspectives on the Yi of Southwest China.* London: University of California Press.

Harrison, P. (2004) *Elements of Pantheism.* Coral Springs, FL: Llumina Press.

Harvey, G. (2005) *Animism: Respecting the Living World.* New York: Columbia University Press.

Hattaway, P. (2000) *Operation China: Introducing All the Peoples of China.* Carlisle, UK: Piquant.

He Hong, Mu, X., and Kissya, E. (2010) *Indigenous Knowledge and Customary Law in Natural Resource Management: Experiences in Yunnan, China and Haruku, Indonesia: International Work Group for Indigenous Affairs (IWGIA).* Chiang Mai: Asia Indigenous Peoples Pact (AIPP) Foundation.

Hess, C. (2008) *Mapping the New Commons.* Presented at the Twelfth Biennial Conference of the International Association for the Study of the Commons, Cheltenham, UK, 14–18 July.

Hinnells, J.R. (1997) *The Penguin Dictionary of Religions.* 2nd Edition. London: Penguin Books.

Hitchcock, J.T. and Jones, R. (eds.) (1976) *Spirit Possession in the Nepal Himalayas.* Warminster: Aris and Phillips.

Hou, Y. (2016) 'Ritual and Cultural Revival at Tuvan Sacred Natural Sites Supports Indigenous Governance and Conservation of Nature in China'. in *Asian Sacred Natural Sites: Philosophy and Practice in Protected Areas and Conservation.* ed. by Verschuuren, B. and Furuta, N. London & New York: Routledge & Earthscan, 286–296.

Hou v. BLNR (2016) *Mauna Kea Anaina Hou v. Board of Land and Natural Resources SCOT-16-0000788*. Honolulu: Supreme Court of Hawaii.

Hou v. BLNR (2015) *Hou v Board of Land and Natural Resources SCAP-14-0000873*. Honolulu: Supreme Court of Hawaii.

Huber, T. (1999) *The Cult of Pure Crystal Mountain: Popular Pilgrimage and Visionary Landscape in Southeast Tibet*. vol. a. Oxford: Oxford University Press.

Hultkrantz, A. (1961) *The Supernatural Owners of Nature: Nordic Symposium on the Religious Conceptions of Ruling Spirits (Genii Loci, Genii Speciei) and Allied Concepts*. Stockholm: Almqvist & Wiksell.

Huber, T. (1997) 'Green Tibetans: A Brief Social History'. in Tibetan Culture in the Diaspora. ed. by Korom, F. ed. Wien: Verlag der Osterreichischien Akademie der Wissenschaften, 103–119.

ICJ (1960) *Tibet and the Chinese People's Republic: A Report to the International Commission of Jurists by Its Legal Inquiry Committee on Tibet*. Geneva: International Commission of Jurists.

Illich, I. (1983) 'Silence Is a Commons'. *The CoEvolution Quarterly* 40 (Winter), 4–8.

Ingold, T. (2006) 'Rethinking the Animate, Re-Animating Thought'. *Ethnos* 71 (11), 9–20.

Ingold, T. (2000) *The Perception of the Environment: Essays in Livelihood, Dwelling and Skill*. Abingdon: Routledge.

Insoll, T. (2011) *The Oxford Handbook of the Archeology of Ritual and Religion*. Oxford: Oxford University Press.

Issitt, M.L. and Main, C. (2014) *Hidden Religion: The Greatest Mysteries and Symbols of the World's Religious Beliefs: The Greatest Mysteries and Symbols of the World's Religious Beliefs*. Santa Barbara: ABC-CLIO.

IUCN (2017) *IUCN World Heritage Evaluations 2017: IUCN Evaluations of Nominations of Natural and Mixed Properties to the World Heritage List*. Gland, Switzerland: IUCN.

Jacek (2014) *Mahoning Creek below Kase Run* https://commons.wikimedia.org/w/index.php?curid=34170032

Jacobsen, T. (2016) *Re-Envisioning Sovereignty: The End of Westphalia?* Abingdon: Routledge.

James, W. (1977) *A Pluralistic Universe*. vol. 4. London: Harvard University Press.

Jamieson, M. (2009) 'Contracts with Satan: Relations with "Spirit Owners" and Apprehensions of the Economy among the Coastal Miskitu of Nicaragua'. *Durham Anthropology Journal* 16 (2), 44–53.

Jinba, T. (2013) *In the Land of the Eastern Queendom: The Politics of Gender and Ethnicity on the Sino-Tibetan Border*. University of Washington Press.

Jinba, 2016, pers. comm., 9 Jan.

Jinba, 2016, pers. comm., 5 Jan.

Johanson, D.C. and Edgar, B. (1996) *From Lucy to Language*. New York City: Simon and Schuster.

Jonas, 2017, pers. comm., 29 Jun.

Juducia y Pas (2009) *Indigenous Emberá Communities Resist Invasion by Multinational Mining Corporation in the Bajo Atrato, Colombia*. Bogata: Juducia y Pas.

KAHEA v UHH (2013) *KAHEA v UHH HA-11–05 TMT Final Decision*. [online] available from <http://dlnr.hawaii.gov/occl/files/2013/08/HA-11-05-TMT-Final-Decision.pdf> [1 June 2018].

Karmay, S.G. (2004) 'A Comparative Study of the Yul Lha Cult in Two Areas and Its Cosmological Aspects'. in *New Horizons in Bon Studies*. ed. by Karmay, S.G. and Yasuhiko Nagano. New Delhi: Saujanya Publications, 383–413.

Karmay, S.G. (1998) *The Arrow and the Spindle: Studies in History, Myths, Rituals and Beliefs in Tibet*. Kathmandu: Mandala Book Point.

Karmay, S.G. and 長野泰彦 (2008) *A Survey of Bonpo Monasteries and Temples in Tibet and the Himalaya* (Edited by S.G. Karmay and Y. Nagano; Compiled by D. Lhagyal . . ., et al.). New Delhi: Saujanya Publications.

Kelkar, G., Nathan, D., and Walter, P. (2003) *Gender Relations in Forest Societies in Asia*. London: Sage Publications.

Keown, D. and Prebish, C.S. (2013) *Encyclopedia of Buddhism*. Abingdon: Routledge.

Kernan, M. (2013) 'The Displacement of Tibetan Nomads, International Law and the Loss of Global Indigenous Culture'. *Global Policy Journal* (March).

Kiely, J. and Jessup, J.B. (2016) *Recovering Buddhism in Modern China*. New York: Columbia University Press.

Ktunaxa Nation v. British Columbia (Forests) (2017) *Ktunaxa Nation v. British Columbia (Forests) 2017 SCC 54 36664*. available from <http://canlii.ca/t/hmtxn> [6 November 2017].

La Follette, C. and Maser, C. (2017) *Sustainability and the Rights of Nature: An Introduction*. Boca Raton: CRC Press.

Laidlaw, D. (2017) *Silencing the Qat'muk Grizzly Bear Spirit*. available from <https://ablawg.ca/2017/11/06/silencing-the-qatmuk-grizzly-bear-spirit/> [6 November 2017].

Landerer, E. (2009) *Personhood and Companionship among Evenki and Their Reindeer in Eastern Siberia*. [online] available from <http://munin.uit.no/handle/10037/2241> [10 November 2016].

Lane, F. (1994) 'The Warrior Tribes of Kham'. *Asiaweek* (March 2), 30–38.

Latour, B. (2012) *We Have Never Been Modern*. London: Harvard University Press.

Lausche, B.J. and Burhenne-Guilmin, F. (2011) *Guidelines for Protected Areas Legislation*. vol. 81. Gland, Switzerland: IUCN.

Leroy Little Bear, 2016, pers. comm., 26 Nov.

Lhamo Tsheskyid (2012) *Freeing Trees {ཚེ་རིང་དབང་འཕེལ་ཤོང}*. available from <www.amdotibet.cn/html/jd/2012-04/12493.html> [1 June 2018].

Lightfoot, W.E. (1986) 'Regional Folkloristics'. in *Handbook of American Folklore*. ed. by Dorson, R. Bloomington: Indiana University Press, 183–193.

Limusishiden (2014) 'An Abandoned Mountain Deity'. *Asian Highlands Perspectives* 35, 159–193.

Luo, Z. (1991) *Religion under Socialism in China*. Armonk: ME Sharpe.

Lye, T.-P. (2005) 'The Meanings of Trees: Forest and Identity for the Batek of Pahang, Malaysia'. *The Asia Pacific Journal of Anthropology* 6 (3), 249–261.

Lynch, O. and Alcorn, J. (1993) 'Tenurial Rights and Community-Based Conservation'. in *Natural Connections Perspectives in Community Based Conservation*. ed. by Western, D., Wright, M., and Strum, D. Washington, DC: Island Press, 373–392.

Lyver, P.O. and Moller, H. (2010) 'An Alternative Reality: Maori Spiritual Guardianship of New Zealand's Native Birds'. *Ethno-Ornithology: Birds, Indigenous Peoples, Culture and Society* 241–264.

Makley, C.E. (2007) *The Violence of Liberation: Gender and Tibetan Buddhist Revival in Post-Mao China.* Berkeley: University of California Press.

Marshall, P.A. and Johnson, J.E. (2007) 'The Great Barrier Reef and Climate Change: Vulnerability and Management Implications'. *Climate Change and the Great Barrier Reef: Great Barrier Reef Marine Park Authority and the Australian Greenhouse Office, Australia* 774–801.

Marshall, S. and Cooke, S. (1997) *Tibet Outside the TAR (CD)*. Tibet: Alliance for Research.

Martin, C. (1982) *Keepers of the Game: Indian-Animal Relationships and the Fur Trade.* Berkeley: University of California Press.

Martin, G. (2012) 'Playing the Matrix: The Fate of Biocultural Diversity in Community Governance and Management of Protected Areas'. in *Why Do We Value Diversity? Biocultural Diversity in a Global Context RCC Perspectives* [online]. ed. by Martin, G., Mincyte, D., and Munster, U. vol. 9, 59–64. http://www.environment andsociety.org/sites/default/files/layout_issue_9_final_web.pdf

Mathews, F. (1995) *Ecology and Democracy.* Hove: Psychology Press.

McDowell, J.H. (2015) *Sayings of the Ancestors: The Spiritual Life of the Sibundoy Indians.* Lexington: University Press of Kentucky.

McKay, A. (2013) *Pilgrimage in Tibet.* Richmond: Curzon Press.

Mehta-Jones, S. (2005) *Life in Ancient Rome.* New York: Crabtree Publishers.

Meyer, M.C., Aldenderfer, M.S., Wang, Z., Hoffmann, D.L., Dahl, J.A., Degering, D., Haas, W.R., and Schlütz, F. (2017) 'Permanent Human Occupation of the Central Tibetan Plateau in the Early Holocene'. *Science* 355 (6320), 64–67.

MHURD (2016) *Qinghai Hoh Xil: World Heritage Nomination-Natural Heritage: China.* Beijing: The Ministry of Housing and Urban-Rural Development, PRC.

Miglani v State of Uttarakhand (2017) *Miglani v State of Uttarakhand (2017) Writ Petition (PIL) No. 140 of 2015 Uttarakhand High Court, Nainital.* https://indiank anoon.org/doc/92201770/

Miller, A.M. and Davidson-Hunt, I. (2010) 'Fire, Agency and Scale in the Creation of Aboriginal Cultural Landscapes'. *Human Ecology* 38 (3), 401–414.

Miller, D.J. (2008) *Drokpa: Nomads of the Tibetan Plateau and Himalaya.* Kathmandu: Vajra Publications.

Mills, M. (2003) *Identity, Ritual and State in Tibetan Buddhism: The Foundations of Authority in Gelukpa Monasticism.* London: Routledge.

Minh-Ha, T.T. (2014) *When the Moon Waxes Red: Representation, Gender and Cultural Politics.* Abingdon: Routledge.

Missett, B. (2008) *Soul Theft: How Religions Seized Control of Humanity's Spiritual Nature.* Bloomington: AuthorHouse.

MKAH v BLNR (SOH) (2013) *Mauna Kea Anaina Hou and Others v Board of Land and Natural Resources, State of Hawaii and Others: Re Conservation District Use Permit (CDUP) HA-3568 for the Thirty Meter Telescope at the Mauna Kea Science Reserve, Ka'ohe Mauka, Hamakua District, Island of Hawaii, TMK (3) 4-4-015:009.* https://caselaw.findlaw.com/hi-supreme-court/1719845.html

Modéer, K.A. (2016) 'Sami Law in Late Modern Legal Contexts'. in *Indigenous Rights in Scandinavia: Autonomous Sami Law*. ed. by Allard, C. and Skogvang, S. Abingdon: Routledge, 53–64.

Montejo, V. (2008) 'Mayan Religion (Central America)'. in *Encyclopedia of Religion and Nature*. ed. by Taylor, B. London: A&C Black, 1059–1062.

Morrison, R. (1995) *Ecological Democracy*. Boston: South End Press.

Muhlhausler, P. (2002) *Linguistic Ecology: Language Change and Linguistic Imperialism in the Pacific Rim*. Abingdon: Routledge.

Mukherjea, B.K. and Sen, A.C. (2013) *The Hindu Law of Religious and Charitable Trust*. Kolkata: Eastern Law House.

Mullick v. Mullick (1925) *Pramatha Nath Mullick v. Pradhyumna Kumar Mullick and Another (PC): 1925 AIR (PC) 139: 1925(52) L.R.-I.A. 245*. Mumbai: High Court (Privy Council).

Mullin, G.H. (2005) *The Second Dalai Lama: His Life and Teachings*. Boulder, CO: Snow Lion Publications.

Myers, B. (1994) 'What's Going On'. *MARC Newsletter* 94 (3).

Myers, N., Mittermeier, R., Mittermeier, C., da Fonseca, G., and Kent, J. (2000) 'Biodiversity Hotspots for Conservation Priorities'. *Nature* 403, 853–858.

Myers, S. (2017) *China Is Challenged on Bid for Unesco Heritage Status in Tibetan Area*. available from www.nytimes.com/2017/07/06/world/asia/china-tibet-unesco.html [22 June 2018].

Nadasdy, P. (2005) 'The Anti-Politics of TEK: The Institutionalization of Co-Management Discourse and Practice'. *Anthropologica* 47 (2), 215–232.

Naffine, N. (2009) *Law's Meaning of Life: Philosophy, Religion, Darwin and the Legal Person*. London: Bloomsbury Publishing.

Nagendra, H. and Ostrom, E. (2012) 'Polycentric Governance of Multifunctional Forested Landscapes'. *International Journal of the Commons* [online] 6 (2), 104–133.

Ngenpin, A.M.L. (n.d.) *The Mapuche Universe: Equilibrium and Harmony*. [online] available from <www.mapuche.info/mapuint/mapuniv030530.html> [8 November 2016].

Nightingale, A. (2006) *A Forest Community or Community Forestry? Beliefs, Meanings and Nature in North-Western Nepal*. Edinburgh: Institute of Geography, School of Geosciences, University of Edinburgh.

Nikolic, M. (2017) *Minoritarian Ecologies: Performance before a More-Than-Human World*. PhD Thesis. London: University of Westminster.

Nisbet, R. (2014) *The Quest for Community*. New York City: Open Road Media.

NIT and The Crown (2017) *Ngā Iwi o Taranaki and the Crown Record of Understanding for Mount Taranaki, Pouakai and the Kaitake Ranges*. Wellington: New Zealand Government.

Northcott, M.S. (1996) *The Environment and Christian Ethics*. vol. 10. Cambridge: Cambridge University Press.

Nuccetelli, S., Schutte, O., and Bueno, O. (2013) *A Companion to Latin American Philosophy*. New Hoboken: Wiley.

OIA Organización Indígena de Antioquia (undated) *Sitios Sagrados Naturales (SNS)*. [online] available from <www.arcgis.com/apps/MapTour/index.html?appid=21142177e0d448d59a9dc7de4c5d2c36> [7 July 2017].

Olsen, B. (2000) *Sacred Places: 101 Spiritual Sites around the World*. San Francisco: CCC Publishing.

Oriel, E. (2014) 'Whom Would Animals Designate as "Persons"? On Avoiding Anthropocentrism and Including Others'. *Journal of Evolution & Technology* 24 (3), 44–59.

O'Riordan, T. (1981) *Environmentalism*. 2nd Edition. London: Pion Ltd.

Ostrom, E. (2015) *Governing the Commons: The Evolution of Institutions for Collective Action*. New York: Cambridge University Press.

Ostrom, E., Gardner, R., Walker, J., and Walker, J. (1994) *Rules, Games, and Common-Pool Resources*. Ann Arbor: University of Michigan Press.

Ostrom, V. (1972) *Polycentricity: Working Paper*. 'Annual M4eeting of the American Political Science Association 1972' [online] held 1972 at Washington Hilton Hotel, Bloomington: Indiana University Press, Washington, DC, 5–9 September.

Ourvan, J. (2016) *The Star Spangled Buddhist: Zen, Tibetan, and Soka Gakkai Buddhism and the Quest for Enlightenment in America*. New York City: Skyhorse Publishing.

Panikkar, R. (1993) *The Cosmotheandric Experience: Emerging Religious Consciousness*. Maryknoll: Orbis Books.

Parajuli, P. (1999) 'Peasant Cosmovisions and Biodiversity: Some Reflections from South Asia'. in *Cultural & Spiritual Values of Biodiversity*. ed. by Posey, D. London: Intermediate Technology Publications & UNEP, 385–388.

Pei Shengji (1993) 'Managing for Biological Diversity Conservation in Temple Yards and Holy Hills'. in *Ethics Religion & Biodiversity*. ed. by Hamilton, L. Cambridge: The White Horse Press, 118–132.

Peissel, M. (1972) *Cavaliers of Kham: The Secret War in Tibet*. London: Heinemann.

Peng, W. (2002) 'Frontier Process Provincial Politics and Movements for Khamba Autonomy during the Republican Period'. in *Khams Pa Histories: Visions of People Place and Authority*. ed. by Epstein, L. Leiden, Boston & Koln: Brill, 57–84.

Petrazycki, L. (2011) *Law and Morality*. Piscataway: Transaction Publishers.

PGE v. GT (2015) *Pennsylvania General Energy Company, Llc V. Grant Township, No. 1:2014cv00209: Document 113 (W.D. Pa. 2015)*. Erie: US District Court.

PGE v. GT (2014) *Pennsylvania General Energy Company v. Grant Township, No. 14–209ERIE, 2015 WL 6001882*. Erie: US District Court.

Plumwood, V. (2002) *Environmental Culture: The Ecological Crisis of Reason*. Hove: Psychology Press.

Plumwood, V. (1993) *Feminism and the Mastery of Nature*. Abingdon: Routledge.

Plurinational State of Bolivia (2010) *Bolivia: Law of the Rights of Mother Earth | Ley de Derechos de La Madre Tierra [No. 071 | December 7, 2010] | Peoples' Agreement*. [online] available from <http://peoplesagreement.org/?p=1651> [29 May 2017].

Posey, D. (ed.) (1999) *Spiritual & Cultural Values of Biodiversity*. London: Intermediate Technology Publications and United Nations Environment Programme – UNEP.

Powers, J. (2007) *Introduction to Tibetan Buddhism*. Boulder, CO: Snow Lion Publications.

Pungetti, G., Oviedo, G., and Hooke, D. (2012) *Sacred Species and Sites: Advances in Biocultural Conservation*. Cambridge: Cambridge University Press.

Punzi, V. (2014) 'Tense Geographies: The Shifting Role of Mountains in Amdo between Religious Rituals and Socio-Political Function'. in *Il Tibet Fra Mito e Realtà [Tibet between Myth and Reality]*. ed. by Lo Bue, E. Firenze: Leo S Olschki, 71–80.

Qi, J. (1998) 'Herdsmen in China to End Nomadic Life'. *Xinhua* (March 18).

Ramble, C. (2008) *The Navel of the Demoness: Tibetan Buddhism and Civil Religion in Highland Nepal*. Oxford: Oxford University Press.

REANCBRN (2011) *Republica Del Ecuador Asamblea Nacional, Comision de La Biodiversidad y RecursosNaturales (2011), Acta de Session No.66*. https://asambleanacional.gov.ec/blogs/comision6/files/2011/07/acta-66.pdf [16 September 2018].

Reece v. Edmonton City (2011) *Tove Reece, Zoocheck Canada Incorporated and People for the Ethical Treatment of Animals, Inc. V City of Edmonton – 2011 ABCA 238*. https://www.animallaw.info/case/reece-v-edmonton-city

Reichel, E. (2012) 'The Landscape in the Cosmoscape, and Sacred Sites and Species among the Tanimuka and Yukuna Amerindian Tribes (North-West Amazon)'. in *Sacred Species and Sites: Advances in Biocultural Conservation*. ed. by Pungetti, G., Oviedo, G., and Hooke, D. Cambridge: Cambridge University Press, 127–151.

Reichel, E. (1992) *Shamanistic Modes for Environmental Accounting in the Colombian Amazon: Lessons from Indigenous Ethno-Ecology for Sustainable Development*. International Symposium on Indigenous Knowledge and Sustainable Development, 20–26 September.

Rios, H. (2016) *F-5 Witness Statement: Hawane Rios*. Hawaii: Board of Land and Natural Resources. available from <https://dlnr.hawaii.gov/mk/files/2016/10/F-5-WDT-Hawane-Rios.pdf> [1 June 2018].

Romain, W.F. (2009) *Shamans of the Lost World: A Cognitive Approach to the Prehistoric Religion of the Ohio Hopewell*. Lanham: AltaMira Press.

Rowcroft, P., Studley, J., and Ward, K. (2006) 'Eliciting Forest Values for Community Plantations and Nature Conservation'. *Forests Trees and Livelihoods* 16, 329–358.

Rutte, C. (2011) 'The Sacred Commons: Conflicts and Solutions of Resource Management in Sacred Natural Sites'. *Biological Conservation* 144 (10), 2387–2394.

Safi, M. (2017) 'Ganges and Yamuna Rivers Granted Same Legal Rights as Human Beings'. *The Guardian*. https://www.theguardian.com/world/2017/mar/21/ganges-and-yamuna-rivers-granted-same-legal-rights-as-human-beings

Salick, J., Amend, A., Anderson, D., Hoffmeister, K., Gunn, B., and Zhendong, F. (2007) 'Tibetan Sacred Sites Conserve Old Growth Trees and Cover in the Eastern Himalayas'. *Biodiversity and Conservation* 16, 693–706.

Salim v State of Utarakhand (2017) *Salim v State of Utarakhand and Others (2017) Writ Petition No. 210 of 2017(M/S) Uttarakhand High Court, Nanital*. https://indiankanoon.org/doc/81629830/

Salmon, E. (2000) Kincentric Ecology: Indigenous Perceptions of the Human Nature Relationship, *Ecological Applications* 10 (5), 13271332.

Salmond, J.W. (1913) *Jurisprudence*. London: Stevens and Haynes.

Samakov, A. and Berkes, F. (2017) 'Spiritual Commons: Sacred Sites as Core of Community-Conserved Areas in Kyrgyzstan'. *International Journal of the Commons* 11 (1).

Samuel, G. (2002) 'The Epic and Nationalism in Tibet'. in *Religion and Biography in China and Tibet*. ed. by Penny, B. Richmond: Curzon Press, 178–188.

Samuel, G. (1993) *Civilized Shamans: Buddhism in Tibetan Societies*. Washington, DC: Smithsonian Institute Press.

Sandars, T.C. (1917) *The Institutes of Justinian*. Clark & The Lawbook Exchange Ltd.

Sarat, A. and Kearns, T.R. (2009) *Law's Violence*. Ann Arbor: University of Michigan Press.

Sax, J.L. (1970) 'The Public Trust Doctrine in Natural Resource Law: Effective Judicial Intervention'. *Michigan Law Review* 68 (3), 471–566.

Schaeffer, K.R., Kapstein, M., and Tuttle, G. (2013) *Sources of Tibetan Tradition*. New York: Columbia University Press.

Schmidt, B.E. and Huskinson, L. (2010) *Spirit Possession and Trance: New Interdisciplinary Perspectives*. London: Bloomsbury Publishing.

Schromen-Wawrin, L. (2018) 'Representing Ecosystems in Court: An Introduction for Practitioners'. *Tulane Environmental Law Journal* 31, 279–291.

Schwartz, R. (1994) *Circle of Protest: Political Ritual in the Tibetan Uprising*. London: Hurst & Co.

Seeland, K. (1993) 'Sanskritisation and Environmental Perception among Tibeto-Burman Speaking Groups'. in *Anthropology of Tibet and the Himalaya*. ed. by Ramble, C. and Brauen, M. Zurich: University of Zurich, 354–363.

Sheleff, L.S. (2013) *The Future of Tradition: Customary Law, Common Law and Legal Pluralism*. Abingdon: Routledge.

Shelton, D. (2015) 'Nature as a Legal Person'. *VertigO – La Revue Électronique En Sciences de l'environnement*, Hors-série 22 [online].

Shen, X., Li, S., Wang, D., and Lu, Z. (2015) 'Viable Contribution of Tibetan Sacred Mountains in Southwestern China to Forest Conservation'. *Conservation Biology* 29 (6), 1518–1526.

Shen, X., Lu, Z., Li, S., and Chen, N. (2012) 'Tibetan Sacred Sites: Understanding the Traditional Management System and Its Role in Modern Conservation'. *Ecology and Society* 17 (2) [online].

Sierra Club v. Morton (1972) *Sierra Club v Morton (1972) 405 US 727*. Washington, DC: US Supreme Court.

Singh, N. (2017) 'Becoming a Commoner: The Commons as Sites for Affective Socio-Nature Encounters and Cobecomings'. *Ephemera* 17 (4), 751–776.

Singh, N. (ed.) (2009) *The Secret Abode of Fireflies: Loving and Losing Spaces of Nature in the City*. New Delhi: Youthreach.

Sobrevila, C. (2008) *The Role of Indigenous Peoples in Biodiversity Conservation: The Natural but Often Forgotten Partners*. World Bank.

Sochaczewski, P, 2017, pers. comm., 3 Sept.

Solon, P. (2014) *Rights of Mother Earth: Notes for Debate*. [online] available from <rights-of-mother-earth-a4-small-file-size.pdf> [1 June 2018].

Sponsel, L. (2012) *Spiritual Ecology: A Quiet Revolution*. Santa Barbara: ABC-CLIO.

Sponsel, L. (2007) 'Animism'. in *Encyclopedia of Environment and Society*. ed. by Robbins, P. Thousand Oaks: Sage Publications, 49–50.

Stahler-Sholk, R. (2000) 'A World in Which Many Worlds Fit: Zapatista Responses to Globalization'. *Latin American Studies Association, Miami, Florida. Retrieved August* 15, 1–16.

Stalin, J. (1951) *Marxism and Linguistics*. New York: International Publishers.

State of Uttarakhand v Salim (2017) *Petition(s) for Special Leave to Appeal (C) No(s). 016879/2017 (Arising out of Impugned Final Judgment and Order Dated 20–03–2017 in WP(PIL) No. 126/2014)*. Nanital: High Court of Uttarakhand.

Stavru, S. (2016) 'Rights of Nature: Is There a Place for Them in the Legal Theory and Practice?'. *Sociological Problems* 1–2, 146–166.

Stein, R. (1972) *Tibetan Civilization*. London: Faber.

Stevens, S. (ed.) (1997) *Conservation through Cultural Survival: Indigenous People and Protected Areas*. Washington, DC: Island Press.

Stevens, S. (1993) *Claiming the High Ground: Sherpas Subsistence and Environmental Change in the Highest Himalaya*. Berkeley: University of California Press.

Stone, C.D. (2010) *Should Trees Have Standing?: Law, Morality, and the Environment*. Oxford: Oxford University Press.

Stone, C.D. (1972) 'Should Trees Have Standing: Toward Legal Rights for Natural Objects'. *Southern California Law Review* 45, 450–501.

Studley, J. (2017a) *The Ritual Protection of Sacred Natural Sites on the Tibetan Plateau and the Optimisation of Lay Participation*. Unpublished manuscript.

Studley, J. (2017b) *Why Shouldn't Sacred Natural Sites Be Declared as Juristic Persons Predicated on Spiritual Governance?* [online] available from <http://sacred naturalsites.org/2017/06/declaring-sacred-natural-sites-as-juristic-persons/> [1 June 2018].

Studley, J. (2016) *Is Yundrung Bon Compatible with the Tibetan Gzhi Bdag Cult*. available from <www.academia.edu/25504458/Is_Yundrung_Bon_compatible_ with_the_Tibetan_gzhi_bdag_cult> [9 December 2016].

Studley, J. (2014) *Gzhi Bdag: Custodians of the Tibetan Spiritscape: A Bio-Cultural Audit of Sacred Natural Sites in NW Yunnan (with Special Reference to the Yubeng Valley)*. Hong Kong: China Exploration and Research Society.

Studley, J. (2012) 'Territorial Cults as a Paradigm of Place in Tibet'. in *Making Sense of Place*. ed. by Convery, I., Corsane, G., and Davis, D. Woodbridge: Boydell Press, 219–234.

Studley, J. (2010) 'Uncovering the Intangible Values of Earth Care: Using Cognition to Reveal the Eco-Spiritual Domains and Sacred Values of the Peoples of Eastern Kham'. in *Sacred Natural Sites: Conserving Nature and Culture*. ed. by Verschuuren, B., Wild, R., McNeely, J., and Oviedo, G. London: Earthscan, 107–118.

Studley, J. (2007) *Hearing a Different Drummer: A New Paradigm for "Keepers of the Forest"*. London: IIED.

Studley, J. (2005) *Sustainable Knowledge Systems and Resource Stewardship: In Search of Ethno-Forestry Paradigms for the Indigenous Peoples of Eastern Kham*. PhD Thesis. Loughborough: Loughborough University.

Studley, J. (2004) 'The Challenge of Ethno-Forestry: The Predicament of Traditional Local Forest Practices around Lugu Lake in China'. *Trees: Journal of the International Tree Foundation* 64, 16–17.

Studley, J. (2003) *The History of Kham*. available from <http://thunderbolt.me.uk/ KhamHistory.pdf> [31 May 2018].

Studley, J. (1999) 'Environmental Degradation in Southwest China'. *China Review* (Spring), 28–33.

Studley, J. and Awang, J. (2016) 'Creating New Discursive Terrain for the Custodians of the Tibetan Spiritscapes of North West Yunnan'. in *Asian Sacred Natural Sites: Philosophy and Practice in Protected Areas and Conservation*. ed. by Verschuuren, B. and Furuta, N. Abingdon: Routledge, 271–285.

Studley, J. and Bleisch, W. (2018) 'Juristic Personhood for Sacred Natural Sites: A Potential Means for Protecting Nature'. *Parks* 24 (1), 81–96.

Sun, H. (1990) 'Languages of the Ethnic Corridor in Western Sichuan'. *Linguistics of the Tibeto-Burman Area* 13 (1), 1–31.

Swanson, P. (1993) 'Zen Is Not Buddhism: Recent Japanese Critiques of Buddha-Nature'. *Numen* 40 (2), 115–149.

Tacey, D. (2013) *Gods and Diseases: Making Sense of Our Physical and Mental Wellbeing*. Abingdon: Routledge.

Teasdale, W. (2010) *The Mystic Heart: Discovering a Universal Spirituality in the World's Religions*. Novato: New World Library.

Tengö, M., Johansson, K., Rakotondrasoa, F., Lundberg, J., Andriamaherilala, J.-A., Rakotoarisoa, J.-A., and Elmqvist, T. (2007) 'Taboos and Forest Governance: Informal Protection of Hot Spot Dry Forest in Southern Madagascar'. *AMBIO: A Journal of the Human Environment* 36 (8), 683–691.

Thiselton, A.C. (2005) *A Concise Encyclopedia of the Philosophy of Religion*. Ada: Baker Academic.

Times of India (2017) *Supreme Court Stays Uttarakhand High Court's Order Declaring Ganga and Yamuna "Living Entities"*. Mumbai: Times of India.

Tippett, A.R. (1973) *Aspects of Pacific Ethnohistory*. Pasadena: William Carey Library Pub.

Tiwari, S.K. (2002) *Tribal Roots of Hinduism*. New Delhi: Sarup & Sons Publishing.

TNZPCC – The New Zealand Parliament Counsel Office (2016) *Te Awa Tupua (Whanganui River Claims Settlement) Bill* [online]. Wellington, 129–121.

TNZPCC – The New Zealand Parliamentary Counsel Office (2014) *Te Urewera Act 2014 No 51, Public Act: New Zealand Legislation*. Wellington.

Totten, T. (2015) 'Should Elephants Have Standing'. *Western Journal of Legal Studies* 6, 1.

Trask, M. (2007) 'Indigenous Women and Traditional Knowledge: Reciprocity Is the Way of Balance'. in *Women and the Gift Economy: A Radically Different Worldview Is Possible*. ed. by Vaughan, G. Toronto: Innana Publications, 293–300.

Tsering, R. (2016) 'Labtse Construction and Differentiation in Rural Amdo'. *Revue d'Etudes Tibetaines* 37 (December), 451–468.

Tsering, T. (1985) 'Nag Ron Mgon Po Rnam Rgyal: A 19th Century Khams-Pa Warrior'. in *Soundings in Tibetan Civilization*. ed. by Aziz, B. and Kapstein, M. New Delhi: Manohar, 196–214.

Turnbull, C.M. (1976) *Wayward Servants: The Two Worlds of the African Pygmies*. Westport: Greenwood Pub Group.

Tyżlik-Carver, M. (2016) *Curating in/as Commons Posthuman Curating and Computational Cultures*. [online] available from <www.academia.edu/29844696/Curating_in_as_Common_s_Posthuman_Curating_and_Computational_Cultures> [1 June 2018].

UNDRIP (2007) *UN General Assembly, United Nations Declaration on the Rights of Indigenous Peoples: Resolution/Adopted by the General Assembly, 2 October 2007, A/RES/61/295*. New York: UNDRIP.

UNDRIP (1993) *UN Draft Universal Declaration on the Rights of Indigenous Peoples, 23 August 1993, UN Doc. E/CN.4/Sub.2/1993/29; UN Doc. E/CN.4/Sub.2/1994/2/ Add.1. UN*. New York: UNDRIP.

UNESCAP (2009) *What Is Good Governance?* Bangkok: UNESCAP.

United Nations General Assembly (2016a) *Harmony with Nature A/71/266*. New York: UN.

United Nations General Assembly (2016b) *United Nations Official Document A/ RES/70/1 Transforming Our World*. New York: UN.

United Nations (2015) *United Nations Official Document A/RES/70/208 Harmony with Nature*. New York: UN.

Vaccari, A. (2012) 'Dissolving Nature: How Descartes Made Us Posthuman'. *Techné: Research in Philosophy and Technology* 16 (2), 138–186.

Van Rheenen, G. (2013) *Communicating Christ in Animistic Contexts*. Pasadena: William Carey Library Pub.

van Spengen, W. (2002) 'Frontier History of Southern Kham: Banditry and War in the Multi-Ethnic Fringe Lands of Chatring Mili and Gyethang 1890–1940'. in *Khams Pa Histories: Visions of People Place and Authority*. ed. by Epstein, L. Leiden, Boston & Koln: Brill, 7–29.

Verschuuren, B. (2007) *Believing Is Seeing: Integrating Cultural and Spiritual Values in Conservation Management*. Gland: Foundation for Sustainable Development, The Netherlands and IUCN, Gland.

Verschuuren, B., Wild, R., McNeely, J., and Oviedo, G. (2010) *Sacred Natural Sites: Conserving Nature and Culture*. London: Earthscan.

Wade v Kramer (1984) *Wade v Kramer (1984) 121 Ill. App.3d 377 (Ill. App. Ct. 1984) | California Eastern District Court*. https://www.leagle.com/decision/1984 498121illapp3d3771446

Walker, A.R. (2011) 'From Spirits of the Wilderness to Lords of the Place and Guardians of the Village and Farmlands: Mountains and Their Spirits in Traditional Lahu Cosmography, Belief, and Ritual Practice'. *Anthropos* 110 (2), 359–378.

Wallace, A. (2013) *Religion: An Anthropological View*. New York City: Random House.

Washington, H., Taylor, B., Kopnina, H., Cryer, P., and Piccolo, J. (n.d.) *A Statement of Commitment to Ecocentrism*. [online] available from <www.ecologicalcitizen. net/statement-of-ecocentrism.php#top> [7 April 2018].

Watts, V. (2013) 'Indigenous Place-Thought and Agency amongst Humans and Non Humans (First Woman and Sky Woman Go on a European World Tour!)'. *Decolonization: Indigeneity, Education & Society* 2 (1) [online].

WCC World Council of Churches (2009) *Joint Declaration of Indigenous Churches: Eighth Period of Sessions of the United Nations Permanent Forum on Indigenous Issues* https://www.oikoumene.org/en/resources/documents/wcc-programmes/unity-mission-evangelism-and-spirituality/just-and-inclusive-communities/indigenous-people/joint-declaration-of-indigenous-churches-at-un-forum [16 September 2018].

Weston, B.H. and Bollier, D. (2013) *Green Governance: Ecological Survival, Human Rights, and the Law of the Commons*. Cambridge: Cambridge University Press.

Wheeler V DPGEL (2011) *Wheeler y Huddle c. Director de La Procuraduria General Del Estadode Loja (2011)Juicio, No. 11121–2011–10, Casillero No. 826*.

Whitehead, A. (2013) *Religious Statues and Personhood: Testing the Role of Materiality*. London: A&C Black.

Whitt, L. (2009) *Science, Colonialism, and Indigenous Peoples*. Cambridge: Cambridge University Press.

Wilber, K. (2001) *Sex, Ecology, Spirituality: The Spirit of Evolution*. Boulder, CO: Shambhala Publications.

Wild, R. and McLeod, C. (2008) *Sacred Natural Sites: Guidelines for Protected Area Managers*. Gland, Switzerland & Paris, France: IUCN and UNESCO.

Wilmshurst, J.M., Higham, T.F., Allen, H., Johns, D., and Phillips, C. (2004) 'Early Maori Settlement Impacts in Northern Coastal Taranaki, New Zealand'. *New Zealand Journal of Ecology* 167–179.

Woodhouse, E., Mills, M.A., McGowan, P.J., and Milner-Gulland, E.J. (2015) 'Religious Relationships with the Environment in a Tibetan Rural Community: Interactions and Contrasts with Popular Notions of Indigenous Environmentalism'. *Human Ecology* 43 (2), 295–307.

Wright, R.M. (2013) *Mysteries of the Jaguar Shamans of the Northwest Amazon*. Lincoln: University of Nebraska Press.

Xu, J., Ma, E., Tashi, D., Fu, Y., Lu, Z., and Melick, D. (2005) 'Integrating Sacred Knowledge for Conservation: Cultures and Landscapes in Southwest China'. *Ecology and Society* 10 (2).

Yang Fuquan (2003) 'The Fireplace: Gender and Culture among Yunnan Nationalities'. in *Gender Relations in Forest Societies in Asia: Patriarchy at Odds*. ed. by Kelkar, G., Nathan, D., and Walter, P. London: Sage Publications, 61–77.

Yeh, E 2016, pers. comm., 6 Oct.

Yeh, E. and Lama, K. (2015) *Shielding the Mountains: Study Guide*. available from <http://tibetsacredmountain.org/wp-content/uploads/doc/StudyGuide.pdf> [1 June 2018].

Yü, D.S. (2015) *Mindscaping the Landscape of Tibet: Place, Memorability, Ecoaesthetics*. vol. 60. Berlin: Walter de Gruyter GmbH & Co KG.

Zangpo, N. (2002) *Guru Rinpoche: His Life and Times*. Boulder, CO: Snow Lion Publications.

Zevik, E. (2002) 'First Look: The Qiang People of Sichuan'. *Asian Anthropology* 1 (1), 195–206.

Zhang, Z. (2003) *Tibetans' Religious Belief in Holy Mountain and Eco-Friendly Traditional Style of Production and Life at Yubeng Village, Deqin County*. Kunming: Yunnan Academy of Social Science.

Zhong Yun Zhang (2007) *Research of Belief of Sacred Mountains and Villagers Livelihoods*. Kunming: Yunnan Academy of Social Science.

Zion, J.W. (1988) 'Searching for Indian Common Law'. in *Indigenous Law and the State*. ed. by Morse, B. and Woodman, G. Dordrecht: Foris Publications, 121–148.

Index